CONTENTS

The true story of a 10 year old child sex trafficking survivor saved by murder

SPECIAL KINDA BR♥KEN

Gabrielle Monroe
artwork by Breslyn PSB

Hardcover: unavailable at this time
Paperback: 978-1-7379182-2-6
Audiobook: unavailable at this time
Ebook: 978-1-7379182-1-9

First digital/paperback edition September, 13 2020

Cover art by Breslyn PSB

All Rights Reserved

Printed by Amazon in the USA.

Gabrielle Monroe
322 Mall Blvd. #213
Monroeville, PA 15146

GabrielleMonroe.com

Special Kinda Broken

Most people have heard of child sex trafficking.

Author, Gabrielle Monroe, has lived through it.

Sex trafficking is a form of rape that is rarely discussed. It is a hard form of abuse to talk about. Sex trafficking goes beyond rape; it is a vicious form of sexual abuse for the financial benefits of one's abuser. When you're only 9 years old, how do you end your sex trafficking abuse and survive?

In this book, you will find experiences from Gabrielle's childhood sex trafficking abuse, between ages 9-10. You will also find reflections that raise many questions about sex trafficking and provide solutions to both protect sex trafficking victims and survivors as well as prevent sex trafficking before this vile form of rape begins.

Special Kinda Broken walks you through prepubescent child sex trafficking abuse that leaves a lifetime of barriers and obstacles survivors face.

In 1990 there wasn't a term for the type of abuse I was experiencing. I was being traded to grown men in exchange for ice cream money, bill payment and substances. I was only 9 years old when adult men started raping me.

Today we call this form of abuse child sex trafficking. Sex trafficking is a form of rape.

Join me as I recount many instances of abuse I experienced at age 9 - 10 and continue reading as I explore where the system failed me as a young child and how I could have been supported.

You will find more questions than answers as you read. Jot

them down and send them to me if you wish, I would love to hear your thoughts and comments. GabrielleMonroe.com

You will feel emotions. Feel them, acknowledge them, let them go.

Remember your favorite self care routines as you read through this book. Taking care of your mental health is vital as we wade through the murky waters of how to protect children and prevent sex trafficking.

I survived.

I'm a special kinda broken, I'm never going to be ok and that's ok.

Thanks for joining as I recount my journey on how I survived horrific sexual abuse, known as sex trafficking, when I was only 9 years old.

Thank You

to my friends, family and loved ones...

Thank You for supporting me.

Thank You for being a part of my world.

Thank You for loving me.

Special Kinda Broken

Sometimes you are so broken you can't be
fixed. I'm that kind of broken.

I'm a special kinda broken. I'll never be ok, and that's ok.

Special Kinda Broken recounts 7 experiences of
abuse I endured as a child. Violence, sex trafficking,
murder and more shaped my young life creating a
ripple effect of cracks that aren't being healed.

You will have more questions than answers when you are
finished reading. It's time to have the hard conversations
on how to end child sex trafficking abuse. Sex trafficking
is a form of rape we much protect our children from.

You can purchase Special Kinda Broken today
for only $1.99 on Amazon.

Find the direct link at GabrielleMonroe.com on 09/13/2021.

Read and pass it on.

Share with your friends.

The true story of a 10 year old child sex trafficking survivor saved by murder

SPECIAL KINDA BR🖤KEN

Gabrielle Monroe
artwork by Breslyn PSB

Special Kinda Broken

Open the curtain and peek behind the show
There is a world beautifully broken you don't know

We put on a tough face and hide our tears
We don't ever let them see our worst fears

Beautifully broken, inside and out
Every part of our lives create doubt

Beautifully broken, few will ever see
What's buried deep down inside of me

Putting my pain on a platter to display
Most are shocked to my dismay
There has to be a better way
Maybe you will figure it out some day

Placing your sick desire above my life
Hiding your misdeeds from your wife
You've created so much strife
As you've pushed survivors under the knife

Parading your experts near our door
Forgetting survivors as you hit the floor
Silencing our voices to push your folklore
Labeling us as a childhood whore

Pushing us to recount our abuse
Playing with our minds is so loose
When all else fails you try to seduce
When our story doesn't fit your morals you say we are confused

Promise of resources you extend

Setting up house, playing pretend
Will this bullshit ever end
Our lives, when will you ever defend?

Pawning our blood, tears and pain
For your own twisted, personal gain
Our stories make your business strain
You take what's ours, flushing us down the drain

Beautifully broken, up and down.
I try to smile and only manage a frown

Beautifully broken, molded and dark
They didn't care when they took my spark

They broke me down to build me back
It took all I had not to crack
Each abuse and every attack
Life was hard for me to hack

Molded perfectly to their desire
Pushing me closer to the fire
I was not a whore bought by a buyer
Raped and destroyed for hire

Perfectly open to let more abuse in
What I did wasn't a sin
I was a child needing a win
Cutting and crawling out of my skin

Grown men abused me from the start
Grown men rapists tore my world apart
Detached and alone I longed to depart
Runaway to protect my heart

GABRIELLE MONROE

They took my innocence from me
They decided who I should be
They made sure I'd never be free
Tortured and tormented forever by their toxicity.

Beautifully broken, but not dead
I try to calm my busy head
They instilled so much dread
And laid me out like a Thanksgiving Day spread

Beautifully broken from the start
Dozens of men tore my world apart

Beautifully broken...
Now do you see?

Beautifully broken...
Now it's time to set me free.

Off with Her Fingers

Knives drawn
Little loves fawn

Scared and silent
Why is he so violent?

What I did, I did not know
Why was everything an elaborate show?

Knife to fingers
His evil breath lingers

He would cut deep
Fear I would keep

I couldn't do right
I was just starting this fight

My little life lay on the line
I prayed so hard to send me a sign

My true self broken
My voice went unspoken

I let it happen to my mind
My fear he surely defined

My life was always twisted
My abuse displayed and listed

They saw it written on my face
I needed out of this evil place

Run away, I had to try
Or I would soon have to die

There was no help for young little me

For my life I had to plea

He caught me like a fish out of water
The abuse I endured, you'd never know I was his daughter

There is no help for us to be free
For there are no safe spaces for us to flee.

OFF WITH HER FINGERS

I bit my nails well into adulthood.
It was my go-to coping mechanism.
I bit my nails when I was nervous.
I bit my nails when I was scared.
I bit my nails when I was sad.
I bit my nails when I was stressed.
I bit my nails when I was anxious.
I bit my nails when I felt bad...which was most of my childhood.

I didn't know my dad until I met him at the courthouse. I remember the click clack clicking of my black shiny dress shoes with a ½ inch heel. I felt so grown up with that ½ inch heel. I remember curling my toes inside the shoes and pressing my toes really hard against the ground. I always hated shoes that covered my toes.

Click clack click clack, my foster mom held my hand and told me we were going to meet my dad. If the judge allowed it, I was going to live with him. I didn't know who my dad was. I'm not sure if I had even met my dad before that day at the courthouse.

I bit my nails as I walked. Click clack. Click clack.

My dad was a violent man. The judge should have never granted him custody over me.

He was a person who had mental health difficulties. He was poor. He lacked resources. He was abused as a child. He was sexually abused as a child. He had an on and off relationship with substances. He was a mess. A violent mess. A violent mess filled with rage.

My dad was a violent mess, filled with rage who was granted custody over me when I was only 6 years old.

That day in court, the judge told dad that if he "got clean and married his girlfriend," he would be fit to be my parent.

Dad did ok for a while. Then he fell asleep driving the bread truck and messed up his leg badly; the doctor reintroduced him to his friend, 'substances,' and it all went downhill from there.

It angered dad when I would bite my nails. Several times, I got beaten with the belt for biting them. I couldn't help it. It was, for many many years, my self-soothing technique. I did this well into adulthood until I resorted to getting fake nails. The fake nails are the only cure to my nail biting habit. During the Covid-19 pandemic in 2020, I couldn't get my fake nails filled. Thus, I started biting my nails again at 39 years old.

I'll never forget one particular day when I was living with my dad.

I'd never seen my dad so mad at me. As I mentioned before, when I was a little girl, I would always bite my nails. Sometimes, he would beat me for biting them, but on other occasions, he wouldn't notice or he'd simply ignore me.

That day, dad sat in the chair by the window. He told me to put my hand on the edge of the table, and demonstrated how he wanted me to place my hand: palm spread flat against the table,

fingers spread open.

He then pulled out his knife.

When I was close enough, he grabbed me by my wrist and dragged me to the edge of the table. He slammed my hand on the edge of the table and forced my palm to be flat. He then put the knife on my fingers and started to saw back and forth as he screamed at me for biting my nails.

He was cutting my fingers off.

I looked out the window and pretended I was somewhere else while my mouth begged, "Please daddy, no. I won't bite my fingernails again. Please daddy no, don't cut my fingers off." I was sure I would be dying that day. Death by having my fingers cut off. What a way to die.

I begged for my fingers to be saved.
I promised dad I would never bite them again.

A tear ran down my cheek as the knife pierced my skin and he drew blood. As he was sawing deeper, blood began to come out; it was trickling down my pointer finger, just above the middle knuckle. I wasn't going to have left hand fingers anymore. I looked out the window and cried, as silently as I could. I didn't want to anger daddy more. I didn't need all my fingers, anyways, did I? I could use my other hand.

I cried. He sawed.

Then she saved my fingers.

She stepped in.

She told me to go outside.

I ran. I ran and hid in the yard, behind the old, disconnected satellite dishes. I wiped my bloody fingers on the grass and then licked them clean. I couldn't be a bloody mess; dad would beat me.

I don't know what happened to her that day.

I could hear her screams from inside the house as my dad beat her.

She protected me. She always tried to protect me from my dad.

She saved my fingers. She protected me.

My dad screamed at her, " She is my kid and I'll cut her fucking fingers off if I want to."

He was going to kill her...and then kill me next . I ran to the rickety old shed at the edge of our property. I could still hear my stepmom inside screaming as my dad was taking out his anger on her.

In my head, I kept saying over and over, " Run, run far away, run run."

That's exactly what I did. I ran away.

I ran down the street, sucking my still bleeding fingers. I kept on running. I sat in the fire hall parking lot and cried.

I eventually walked home. I never went further than my boundary of the fire hall at the end of the street,. otherwise Dad would kill me, maybe literally.

On a different occasion, after having received a beating from my dad, I ran away with no intention of coming back.

I wanted to go back and live at my last foster home. There was abuse there, but nothing like the abuse I was enduring physically at the hands of my dad.

A house down the street, the grandma who lived there saved me that day. She would buy me gloves, a hat and a coat every winter. She would give me candy and other yummy treats at the bus stop. She knew I was neglected. If my clothes didn't tell the story, my face did.

She gave me a coloring book, one of those giant ones with hundreds of pages and big box of crayons. The super coloring book became my escape from reality. I would color the pictures and imagine being the animal I was coloring. I would escape from my own reality.

I ran away to her house once; I knocked on her door, crying.

She opened the door. I lied and said I went for a walk and got lost. She cleaned the tears from my face, calmed me, got me a cup of tea and then asked, "How do we get you home?" She took me to the last foster home I lived at.

She didn't question me much, knowing I lived down the street. I think she knew who I was and where I lived and took me away from that hell.

I told my foster parent what my dad had done to me. She fed me and calmed me down and said I would be ok. I had bruises all over my bottom and back.

Then Fief, my foster mom, called Jan, my caseworker at Children's Bureau in Greensburg, Pennsylvania. She told Jan I was covered in bruises but she didn't have a bed for me and couldn't take me back.

A few hours later, my dad showed up to get me.

My dad, my abuser, came to pick me up.

My caseworker, Jan, called my dad, knowing my dad beat me black and blue from neck to bottom.

Children's services never helped me. They sent me right back to my abuser, knowing he abused me.

On another occasion, dad beat me so badly with his belt that I was vomiting uncontrollably. Dad took me to the hospital with some shit story about neighborhood kids beating me up.

Yeah because neighborhood grade school kids beat other grade school kids with a belt?

Dad took me to Monsour Hospital. He threatened me on the way there, saying, "We don't talk to cops or anyone who talks to cops." I was silent.

We arrived at Monsour Hospital.

That place was evil. Pure evil. More about them in the next book on my teen years.

The doctors and nurses talked to my dad. They knew who he was. They knew he beat his girlfriends. They knew he beat me, too.

The cop who came just questioned my dad.

The cop only questioned my dad, who was my abuser.

The cop believed my dad's bullshit story about the neighborhood kids ganging up on me. There were no neighborhood kids within easy walking distance of where I lived. I was the only kid on my street, except for one older kid down the street whom I didn't even know.

The cop had no interest in helping me.

I shook my head in agreement with my abuser, my dad, as he talked to the cop. I didn't dare tattle on my dad because *we don't talk to cops*. If I talked to the cops, dad would probably kill me.

The cop had no desire to help me. He didn't even investigate the "neighborhood kids."
I was just another girl being put in her place by a man. The cop had no desire to hold my dad accountable for beating me.

I survived, fingers intact, body intact, and mind intact to endure the next battle, every time he brought one my way.

Every time he broke me down, I came back stronger and able to endure more abuse.

Every time I hear, " What doesn't kill you, makes you stronger," I want to scream!

I AM FUCKING STRONG ENOUGH, DAMMIT!

Believe children when they speak of abuse. It is time to have the hard conversation that admits that some parents simply should NOT be parents.

A judge decided that my dad would be a fit parent if he stopped using substances and got married.

Neither of these are adequate qualifications of a good parent. The judge's religious morals allowed him to place me in the hands of my dad – an abuser.

My dad was a violent man.

He was in prison for violence before he got custody over me. My dad was still a violent man when he got out of prison.

Jesus saved my dad in prison. The judge liked that.

We need to face reality, some folks simply should not be parents. Some folks should never have access to children.

My dad beat me.

Nobody protected me.

Nobody listened to me.

Nobody cared.

I grew up and broke the generational cycle of abuse in my family. My dad was abused as a child. He grew up and had no access to adequate resources to be sound and to teach him how to break the generational abuse cycle and parent me well.

I ended up enduring a lot of abuse at the will of my dad.

There was no guide, handbook or manual on how to break the evil that was literally beaten or raped into some of us as children.

We need to create this manual. We need to teach broken and abused children how to grow up and break the abuse cycles for the next generation.

In the 80's and early 90's, there was no peer support saying it's ok to fuck up as a parent. Nobody was there to say "Here's what I did to change the mistake I made with my child."

As a society, we hush up our family abuses as a way to "save face" or keep family secrets, secrets.

The secrets that are buried behind walls of abuse and privilege, need to come to light.

We can no longer keep family secrets and protect family abusers.

We must talk about the abuse and find ways to end the abuse for our children and their children. We are quick to cancel and walk away from abusers or ignore the abuse all together. We never take time to teach young folks who were abused as children how to end this generational abuse cycle. **We are expecting broken people to parent and raise unbroken children with no support or guidance on how to achieve this monumental task.**

That will never work.

That will never end child abuse.

We have generation after generation abused as children and growing up without paths to heal and learn how to break the generational abuse cycles for their children.

How do we expect folks to be better when we're always concentrating on the problem and never the solution?

The solution to ending child abuse is a generational solution. We didn't get broken in one generation; we sure as hell will not be fixed in one generation.

Most therapy and other mental health resources take a lifetime learning how to heal. We try to heal over and over again. Healing is not a linear process. We seem to be stuck in the healing phases and never break through and find solutions on how to break the abuse cycle parts of the system.

We don't have that sort of time. It is almost impossible to heal from some forms of childhood abuse.

I'm a special kinda broken. I'll never be ok, and that's ok.

We don't have to wait until we are fixed to break generational abuse cycles.

I did it backwards.

I ignored my own needs and my own pain. I worked on me just enough to survive. Just enough to raise my family. Just enough to end the generational abuse cycle attached to my bloodline. Just enough.

I broke the generational abuse cycle in my family, first, before healing me.

My choices were slim.

I had to break the cycle or I had to give up my baby for adoption.

My children will never know what it's like to experience the pain I endured as a child. I did it. I broke the generational abuse for my children. Never, not once, did I raise a belt to my children. I did not sex traffick my children.

I'm not a perfect mom, but I broke all the generational abuse cycles needed to end generations of child sex trafficking happening to the women from my family.

Now it's time for me to finish healing myself. This book is a part of my healing journey. Thanks for coming along on my journey with me.

This book will provide more questions than answers. It is intended to.

Why aren't we ending child abuse?

Why have we let the "it takes a village" mentality slip away and isolate us as parents? This is the opposite of support needed. Isolation is the secret weapon of abusers.

We need to listen to adults who were abused as children and when they grew up, they ended the abuse cycles for their children.

It's time to question everything about the current system and where it is failing our children. It's time to get the village back together and get training on how to not only hold abusers accountable, but more importantly, help victims heal in a way that they are thriving in life and ending the abuse cycle they were born into.

It's time to ask the hard questions and face the tough realities. It's time to end the abuse, for the children.

As you read, journal your thoughts.

It takes a village. If you're reading this book, you are a member of the village.

It's time for the village to protect the children. It's time for the village to center folks with lived experiences; it's time to learn and grow.

Our children are counting on us.

Everyone deserves to be safe from abusers. Everyone, including children, deserves to be centered in their own life.

It's time to end generational abuse cycles and teach survivors how to heal and break the abuse for their children.

When we infantilize children who are speaking about abuse, we are taking away their voices. Broken children grow up to be broke parents without the support they need.

Believe children when they speak of abuse. Protect children. Nobody deserves to be abused.

Chapter One Summary

Everyone deserves to be safe from abusers. Everyone, including children, deserves to be centered in their own life.

It's time to end generational abuse cycles and teach survivors how to heal and break the abuse for their children.

Believe children when they speak of abuse. Protect children. Nobody deserves to be abused.

Going to Make You a Woman Now

Broken
Abused
Shattered and
Used

Stand up tall.
Don't let them see you fall.

Smile real bright.
Don't let them see you put up a fight.

Grabbed
Groped
Drugged and
Doped

Get your head straight
Before it's too late

Play the game
Keep alive your name

Identity
Lost
Spirits are
Tossed

Fuck with your head
They want you dead

Break your will
For the easy kill

Young
Bruised

Battered and
Misused

Beat you down
Take your crown

Build you back up
Sipping poison from their cup

Lost
Alone
Young and
Grown

Use you as their doll
Whenever they call

Innocence they take
It was never a mistake

Blood
Bright
Fear and
Fright

You're a woman now
No matter the how

Act your place
Or they'll fuck up your face

Darkness
Loved
Forced and
Gloved

Subservient you play
To bring peace to your day

Submit to their need

You must do the deed

Hopeless
Shamed
You are
Blamed

It's not at your door
You're not a childhood whore

You've been abused
You've been terribly used

Head
High

Time to
Fly

Heal your soul
Take back your control

Push out the dark
Take back your bark

Innocent
Child
Feelings are
Filed

Feel the pain
Turn it into gain

Embrace your broke
Take another toke

Free
Spirit
Make em
Fear it

Tell your story
Keep your glory

Shut them down
They will drown

Abused
Healing
How are you
Feeling

Hard to live
How do you forgive

Heal and strive
Let your heart lead the drive

Stand
Tall
Fuck them
All

It's ok if you stumble
Love yourself as you crumble

Keep focus on your goals
You've already paid the costly tolls

Heal
Cry
Pain
Goodbye

Healing is not a straight line
Love yourself, you'll be just fine

Healing isn't easy, it is hard
Your life has forever been scared

Laugh
Live
Love and
Give

Sharing your pain lessens your weight
Sharing your pain lessens your hate

You will inspire others to be free
To live their best life, a beautiful future they will soon see

Share
Harm
Fear will
Disarm

Fear will melt away
As you heal a little more each day

Stumble and stand back up
Share the abundance of liquid in your cup

New
Start
Fixed your
Heart

Put the past behind
Center and calm your mind

Move forward with a good heart
Now it is time for your fresh start

You
Deserve the
Best there is to be.

You
Deserve a

Life that is pain free.

GOING TO MAKE YOU
A WOMAN NOW

T he music was loud. There were a lot of people; so many people that there was nowhere to sit and not much space to navigate the room.

Dad rushed me off to play with a little girl who was my own age.

I didn't have many friends as a kid. I was always awkward and said the wrong things. I tried to fit into different groups and I always failed. I got bullied a lot. Nobody seemed to like me. Not my classmates, not my dad, nobody. All the people who liked me, left me.

We lived in an old gas station that was poorly turned into a 2½ bedroom home. I didn't know we were poor. I didn't even know what being poor was, until kids at school told me. We were too poor to afford a necklace to put my house key on, so my dad tied an old shoelace around my neck. I spent my second grade year crying in the bathroom because the mean kids called me 'shoe lace lady.'
Nobody liked me.

Now dad got me a friend. I had always wanted a friend. Since leaving the foster home, there weren't other kids around very often. Now I was at a party and I had a friend. I was the coolest 9

year old on the block. I was also the only 9 year old on the block. But I didn't care, because I had a friend.

She was a year or so older than me and was way cooler, too. She dressed like a teenager and was so nice to me. And now she was MY friend. She never made fun of me. She was kind to me. We danced and giggled and she showed me how to dance for the men at the party.

She taught me how to dance sexy for men and then ask them for money so I can get ice cream at school. All I had to do was smile pretty, dance and then hold my hand out.

It was easy. I could do this.

Finally, I'd show those kids at school that I wasn't the poor "shoe-lace lady" they called me.

Some of the men would push me away, and I'd feel rejected. I didn't understand why they pushed me away.

But now I understand that all of the men should have pushed me away. Every single one should have said no.

I was only 9 years old.

Some of the men would give us sips of beer. It was always beer. It was nasty but I sipped it anyway and smiled pretty for the men, just as I was taught. Some men would give us their lit cigarette to put in our mouth as we danced for them. One man told me it was 'smokin hot' and I danced "sexy."

I started smoking when I was 9. And I did so daily.

Later, the 'smokin hot' cigarette guy lit my cigarette as he orally raped me and then provided his own release in front of me.

Most of the men enjoyed the way they felt when little girls danced for them -- on them.

My friend, who couldn't have been older than 11 years old, taught me how to sit on men's laps and wiggle my bum. She taught me that some of them didn't like dancing but they'd let you rub their upper leg through their jeans. And by their "upper leg," I mean rubbing their penis through their pants. They would give us a dollar or two for that. The later in the night, the bigger the dollars, and the more handsy some of the men would get.

Night 1

A grown man had both of his hands on my hips; I was sitting on his lap and he was pushing and pulling my hips so I would be grinding harder on his penis. We were in the crowded living room. He did that until my bottom got wet. He pushed me off and gave me 10 bucks, a cigarette and told me to go clean myself up. This man sexually abused me, even though he never raped me.

I was only 9 years old.

I had no clue what was happening.
I had no clue this was abuse.
I had no clue that what the men were doing to me was abuse.

They told me they liked my dancing. I was a natural.

"You are a woman now," they would tell me.

My friend was not "grooming me" for sex trafficking. We were both very young and we were not fucking dogs.

We were children being sexually abused and raped by adult men.

She was getting abused.
She was a sex trafficking victim.
I'm not sure if she would self-identify as a sex trafficking survivor or simply a child rape survivor. I wish she was still alive so I could ask her.

She took her life.

On the very first night a guy I danced for told me that I was about to become a woman when I danced for him, I was excited.

I had no idea that my dreams of being a woman were so drastically different than his.

I dreamt of putting on heels and makeup. Dancing in pretty dresses. Running away from the ball at midnight, losing my shoe, and then my prince finding me and sweeping me off of my feet for all eternity.

Every little kid dreams about being an adult. I was no different. I dreamed of the house I would live in, the man I would marry, the car I would drive and the career I would have.

The first night of my sex trafficking abuse wasn't exactly what I had in mind when thinking about becoming a woman.

Makeup and heels were my dreams.

My rapist came into my bedroom right after dad sent me to bed that night. He told me that my dance moves were good and I was going to become a woman now. He got into my bed and asked if I was ready for him to make me a woman.

I said, "Yes".

He raped me.

I was only 9 years old.

I said, "Yes" and he raped me, in my waterbed. There was a mirror on the ceiling above my waterbed. I watched as he abused me.

At 9 years old, I thought this was ok.

At 9 years old, I thought this is how you become a woman, because my rapist told me so.

This man became a regular rapist who would kiss my wounds before raping me. He would trace the outline of my bruises with his finger and gently kiss each bruise that my dad left on me. He would clean and bandage my cuts. He would also brush my hair and ask me if I wanted him to kill my dad for hurting me.

For months, he asked me if I wanted him to kill my dad for me.

After asking me that question, he would rape me, again. I was raped by this man dozens of times in 1990.

My dad never physically raped me.
My dad was my first sex trafficker. He knew about the men. He allowed it to continue. He benefited off of my rape, mostly with substances. My rapists would pay the bills for my dad and feed him more substances.

Once upon a time, there was a little girl who spent months being raped by multiple grown men to support her dad's substance usage, pay the bill with bonus ice cream money on the side.

She did not live happily ever after.

Instead of happily ever after, she stood up to end child sex trafficking.

She is me. I will forever be a special kinda broken. And that's ok.

Thanks for reading.

This is a good time to remind you that my abuse and pain are not yours. I survived and I am alive. I am never going to be ok and that's ok. I am a special kinda broken.

Take care of your mental well being as you read this book. Self-care is essential. The emotions you feel are real and valid. Don't let them consume you. I survived. I am standing today, to end this dehumanizing, soul crushing form of abuse.

If you're still in sex trafficking abuse, know that it is not your fault. I love you. I'm sorry you're experiencing this. Hang on. Sex trafficking survivor siblings are screaming for folks to listen; hopefully we can scream loud enough to create rights, resources and protections for you. I love you. Stay strong.

It's time to end generational child sexual abuse.

Stop raping children.
Stop touching children.
It's time to talk about it.

The only way we will end child rape and sexual abuse is to teach children how to protect themselves. If they don't know what rape is, how are they suppose to know they are being abused?

Nothing about my childhood abuse was ok. I was not a 9 year old prostitute. Some like to blame the victim to redirect the attention away from their own violence and abuse.

I was a 9 year old being raped by grown men.

I wasn't dressed too sexy.

I wasn't too promiscuous.

I wasn't asking for it.

I didn't want it.

I was only 9 years old...

And I was being raped by grown men.

It's time to end generational and organizational sexual abuse and sex trafficking rape abuse.

Let me say that one more time for the folks in the back...

It's time to end generational and organizational sexual abuse and sex/rape trafficking abuse.

You don't get to create victims because you were harmed as a child.

Generation after generation, I traced my family's sexual violence to my grandfather's generation. Uncle Kuku's basement saw too many violent rapes that destroyed us as young children. Children raped by grown men. This was a family tradition. My dad's side of the family was rife with child sexual abusers. These were middle class men who held leadership positions at their jobs and churches. Some went on to be cops.

Although my dad never sexually abused me himself, he was responsible for my sex trafficking rape abuse.

To put an end to this family tradition of raping children, I had to cut my family off. Nearly all of them cut off, to protect my children.

It's time to talk about how to end generational sexual violence and child sex trafficking, which is a form of rape.

We cannot afford to whisper in the background, warning the little ones to stay away, while allowing known family predators access to take the very life from these children.

Shut them down.
Call them out.
End child rape.

It's time to END generational child sexual abuse -- not just talk about ending it. Don't hide the abuse in your family. Don't hide the abuse within your organizations. Don't throw galas and parties to raise money to "help" raise awareness.

Awareness raised.

Now can we get to the part where we actually help childhood sex trafficking victims and survivors?

Can we speak out about the abuse? Can we collaborate to find way on how to end the abuse? Can we work diligently, together to end the abuse?

Finish this book and move forward centering lived experiences above all other voices. Protect sex trafficking victims and survivors.

Ending child sex trafficking rape and childhood sexual abuse starts with us.

Are you ready to do the hard work?

Teach children what rape is.
Teach children what sex trafficking is.
Give them the knowledge to protect themselves.

Listen to survivors.
Empower survivors.
Center survivors.

And we will end generational sex/rape trafficking abuse.

Chapter Two Summary

It's time to end generational child sexual abuse.

Stop raping children.
Stop touching children.

Stop hiding the family rapists.
Teach children to protect themselves from sexual abuse and rape.

War and Sleep

War abounds
Life is near the end
Cracked and closed
Is there anyone you can send?

Bullets fly
People die
Children cry
Cracks in the sky

Broken and battered
Open to pain
Bruised and tarnished
War is their gain

Lies found
Bells sound
Gather around
Destruction will mound

Seek and find
Crush and destroy
They care little
It's part of their ploy

Blood lost
Lives tossed
Boundaries crossed
Ignoring the cost

Lives changed
Community torn apart
Divide and conquer
It was their goal from the start

Tears shed
Fall on the bed
Pick up your head
You're far from dead

Stand strong
Don't let them push you down
Stand strong
Take back your crown

When war is waged in sexual gaze
It changes us for the rest of our days
We were to young for their abusive slays
It broke us in special kinda ways

I am a special kinda broken
I'll never be ok and that's just fine
I'll never be your token
I'm taking back what's mine

WAR & SLEEP

E verything I knew about how to be a good person came from Mr. Roger's Neighborhood and the Girl Scouts.

Neither platform prepared me for the abuse I endured when I was only 9 years old.

I didn't even know I was being abused.

Sexual violence was not new to me at age 9.
Rape by grown men, however, was a new form of sexual violence added to my life.

And it was painful. Physically, mentally and emotionally painful.

1990.

I was only 9 years old.

There was talk of a war starting in the Middle East.

My young little body was already at war, being sexually abused by grown men, and traded for substances. This happened night after night; party after party; hotel after hotel and parking lot after parking lot.

Being a "woman now" was not fun. It hurt a lot and I cried a lot. I didn't want anyone to see my weakness. I was becoming a woman. I had to be a strong woman.

I needed to be a strong woman to survive.

I didn't even know I was being sexually abused. I didn't know what rape was.

August 2, 1990 - Desert Storm - The invasion of Kuwait.

August 3, 1990

My dad and I visited Gram. The war was all over the television. I remember watching so intently, trying to forget, and trying to ignore the pain in my belly. In an attempt to escape my reality, I imagined being dressed up like a soldier and running with my fellow soldiers. We ran together for hours and then they all raped me. Even in my mind, it was hard to escape the abuse. Most scenarios I'd come up with, ended in rape.

We sat in my Grams living room and watched the news coverage. Dad and Gram talked about the war.

Dad went into the kitchen. Meanwhile, I curled up in Grams lap and told her I didn't feel good. I told her my belly hurt.

Because it did. Inside me, I hurt. And it was the kind of hurt that came with being raped, repeatedly, by multiple grown men.
As I've already mentioned, I didn't know I was being sexually abused.

Gram didn't understand what I was trying to say and I didn't know how to verbalize what was happening.

I couldn't explain. I didn't like "becoming a woman." It hurt. Even though my dad was in the other room, I didn't know what or how to tell my Gram. The best I could manage to say is, "My belly hurts." Because it did.

Gram kissed my forehead and said I felt a little warm. After giving me some applesauce to "settle my belly," a tactic I still use as an adult, Gram walked me to the couch and covered me with a blanket. I hated the scratchy feeling of the blanket. But I hated becoming a woman more. I cringed under the scratchy cover and pretended to be asleep all night. t. I stayed two nights and slept or pretended to be asleep so I didn't have to become a woman for a while. I hurt. I was in pain. I needed a break.

I couldn't go home. So I slept. I was going to die soon. I knew it. I felt it in my heart.

I was Grams pickle, because at the time, pickles were my forever food. One day when
Gram had a family cookout, I ate most of the pickles and hotdogs and corn on the cob because my cousin dared me to. Gram didn't get me; she laughed and hugged me, telling me I was her little pickle.

Gram never abused me. She wouldn't beat me or inappropriately touch me. I was relaxed and comfortable at Grams. I was safe. I was her pickle and she was my Gram, my protector, even if she didn't know.

The day before the war, August 1, 1990 was the first time I tried to kill myself.

I was only 9 years old.

I cut myself deep inside of my thigh, intentionally -- only it wasn't deep enough and I somehow stayed alive. I didn't want to be alive. I couldn't end my abuse. I couldn't even figure out how to end my own life. I was helpless and alone.

In the bathtub, tears running down my face, I tried to kill myself.

And so it began...
I started cutting more often, to manage pain.

I cut. It hurt. It healed. I cut more.

This cycle was endless and lasted well into my teenage years.

One of my abusers would kiss my cut thighs and the bruises that my dad's belt would leave on me. He would bandage up my thighs after kissing them. Once he helped me cut before he bandaged me up.

He told me he'd make me feel all better, and feel so good I'd forget all the pain. He would trace the edges of my bruises with his pointer finger before he'd kiss them. One at a time, trace, kiss, move to the next cut/bruise and repeat. He would stroke my hair and tell me he'd take care of me. He asked me if I was ready to feel better. I said, "Yes." I always told him yes.

What kid wouldn't want to feel better?

Then he'd rape me and give me $1 or $2 to get ice cream at school.

This same abuser offered to kill my dad for me. "Say the word," he would tell me. He said my dad would stop hurting me then. He said he'd take care of me and make me feel all better, forever.

This abuser abused me until my dad was murdered when I was only 10 years old.

Truth be told, he did make me feel better. All the experiences were loving and kind -- something I didn't experience much as a child...until it was time to rape me. He took care of me before he raped me.

He started to bring me snacks. He taught me how to hide them inside my pillowcase so they wouldn't be found as he reminded me to brush any "evidence" meaning crumbs, away. He taught me how to cut inside my thighs so it would be hidden. He taught me how to insert sewing needles into my arms, several at a time. He would remove them one by one. He'd lick and kiss my blood from the needles/razor blades.

He taught me self-harmful behaviors so he could kiss my pain and make me feel all better. He stroked my hair and scratched my back, lightly. He calmed me. He cared for me. He abused me.

After he raped me, he would clean me up and help me into a fresh pair of clean pj's. He brought me a few nightgowns that he liked me to wear. He would brush my hair and tuck me into bed. He would always leave me ice cream money for school. He also kept my dad stocked with substances and even paid bills for my dad.

I was his pretty princess.
He taught how to be a woman.

He took care of me. And he abused me.

He was a grown man who would rape me from summer 1990 until December 1990.

War and sleep...

For two days, I slept or pretended to be asleep so I could heal after my first suicide attempt. My little body was not adjusting to this new form of abuse.

Grown men waged war on me. All I wanted to do was to sleep, and never, ever wake up.

I was well adjusted to my dad's belt, though. That was pain I knew healed. During one particularly violent beating my dad bestowed upon me, I laid face down on the bed, while dad sat on my feet and whipped me with his belt.

On top of that, my little body was being sexually abused often. It needed to rest. My little mind needed to rest, too. If I didn't rest, I would die. I would kill myself. I already tried, and failed but I was sure to try again.

Gram woke me up the second morning. She said if I was not better, she would take me to the hospital.

I couldn't go to the hospital. They wouldn't help. They ignored me when my dad beat me. They wouldn't help now.

I told Gram I was feeling better and asked for some applesauce. Gram scratched my back and played with my hair as she comforted me.

I couldn't deal with life and I wanted to die.

The war started on my little body long before the war in the desert. I had to figure out how to end the abuse. I had to figure out how to survive.

The summer of the war was the same summer my sex trafficking abuse started and I didn't even know I was being raped.

Our children are never too young to talk about rape and rape/ sex trafficking. Our children are never to young to learn how to protect themselves from rape and rape/sex trafficking.

Our children are ALWAYS too young to experience any form of sexual violence.

Silence about sexual violence only perpetuates sexual violence. It allows sexual violence against children to hide in the darkness. If we can't see it, it must not exist.

Silence about sexual violence kills.

It's time to talk about sexual violence, rape and rape/sex trafficking.

I know it's a difficult conversation to have. It hurts to think about children being abused so horribly. It is going to be hard and it is going to hurt. It's going to be messy and painful. However, It has to be done. We must have this messy, hard, horrible conversation on how to really protect our children and prevent rape/sex trafficking in the future.

I didn't understand I was being raped when I was 9 years old. I believed what my abusers told me.

By denying children the basic education of what rape/sex trafficking is, we are leaving them vulnerable to predators. Knowing may not have stopped my abuse as a child. Knowing it wasn't my fault, before I had a child of my own, would have saved me years of self-harm and suicide attempts.

We need to equip children, at all ages, with information and education about rape, sexual violence and rape/sex trafficking. Hiding the hard things in life from children will only protect them if they never experience the hard things in life. When war is waged against children, they are I'll equipped.

When we stop gatekeeping protection information and education, we will protect children.

Our children are never too young to learn how to protect themselves from rape and sex trafficking abuse. To prevent sex trafficking, children need to know what it is.

Our children are always too young to experience rape and sex trafficking abuse.

Chapter Three Summary

Start talking.

Sex trafficking is a form of rape. Children, from a young age, need to know how to identify abuse before they can seek paths to end the abuse. Our children are never too young to learn how to protect themselves from rape and rape/sex trafficking abuse. Our children are always too young to experience rape and rape/sex trafficking abuse.

Three Ohs and a Yeah

He took my voice
I had no choice

He took my will
He made me swallow the fill

He took my spirit
Few would hear it

He took my shine
He took everything good of mine

He took my life
He held the knife

He took my smile
He tasted so vile

He took my dreams
and replaced them with nightmares and screams

He took my mind
He was so unkind

He didn't care about my pain
He only cared for his gain

My aged didn't matter

I was served to him on a platter

I was too young to learn
This sick old man should slowly burn

I was a small child
He should have been profiled

No way was I the first child he raped
I wonder how many futures he misshaped

He knew exactly what he was doing
Young girls like me he was pursuing

Another scar marked deeply on my heart
I was only a little girl doing my part

To end this sickness we must start
Protecting children with all of our heart

THREE OHS AND
A YEAH

D ad was mad. His pain expressed itself as anger. I didn't even have to do anything and he would beat me.

That day, though...

I had never seen dad so mad.

He was tearing through everything in the house. He was looking for something. He was yelling and screaming into the emptiness. Nobody was there to hear him or help him, except me.

He didn't beat me that day. He yelled at me. He yelled to clean the kitchen and make him dinner. He yelled for me to feed my dog and take the garbage out. But he didn't beat me that day.

I did all of my chores, made dinner, cleaned up after dinner, got a bath, brushed my hair, put on my favorite pj's, brushed my teeth, kissed Dad and went to bed.

I was a good girl. I didn't want to make Dad mad.

Dad woke me and told me to get my coat and shoes. We left in the middle of the night, with my snoopy nightgown still on. The nightgown was one of the few things I was allowed to bring to Dad's with me from the foster home....my nightgown, my sock monkey, my stocking holder and the clothes on my body. This nightgown became my security blanket during my abuse. I wore it, washed it and wore it again.

Dad held my hand as we crossed the street and got into a vehicle. Dad was in a better mood now. He opened the back door of a dark colored car, and I hopped in. Dad's friend picked us up. He was one of the men who had been raping me.

They were in the front seat, smoking cigarettes and weed and listening to the radio. I curled into a ball against the door and went back to sleep.

This was not the first time Dad took me out of the house in the middle of the night. We'd go to one of his friends and most times, their spouses would make up the couch for me to sleep on.

The first stop, Dad told me to wait there. Dad and his friend both went inside. I dozed until I heard voices outside the vehicle. Dad and his friend were talking to another man. I couldn't hear what they were saying. I closed my eyes again. I could sleep anywhere when I was a kid.

The car door opened and my head flopped. I was sleeping against the door...I caught myself and sat up and Dad stepped to the side. A man I had never seen before stepped closer to me. He looked at me and backed up.

He started screaming at my dad, " Shes just a fucking kid, what the fuck is wrong with you?”

This man yelling "What the fuck is wrong with you?" at my dad was the very first time I realized I was being abused.

I thought I was a woman, and this is what women do. I thought I was a woman who was supposed to be pleasing men. Why did this man not want me?

They had my head so fucked up. I thought I was a 10 year old woman whose job was to please men.

"What the fuck is wrong with you?" - I thought it was my fault.

I was only 10 years old.

Nothing was wrong with me. I was perfectly molded into their personal rent-a-whore.

I was not a 10 year old prostitute. I was a child being raped by grown men.

At 10, nobody told me I was being raped. I didn't understand what was happening.

This man was so angry, he yelled at my dad and they argued for a few minutes and then the man left.

The "what the fuck is wrong with you" man didn't rape me that night.

He also did nothing to protect me. He yelled at my dad and walked away.

Dad and his friend were now angry. They needed money. They needed drugs.

We drove for a while and stopped in another parking lot. Dad and his friend went inside. Later, they returned, chatting with a man in the parking lot.

Dad opened the door and stepped aside.

This man didn't yell at Dad.

The man came closer. "Oh oh oh yeah," he said in his creepy old man voice as he pushed me to the seat, his penis already out, in hand and ready, and he raped me.

Those four little words, "Oh oh oh yeah," will stick in my mind forever...in his crackling old man voice, he said, "Oh oh oh yeah."

This man had long grey hair, pulled back into a ponytail. He was an old, wrinkled, fragile man.

I'd been raped in the back seat of a car before. My rapists would always be outside of the car. They would have me turn around. They would rape me from behind.

Not this time. This old, nasty man with his wrinkled voice wanted to see my face. He said that. He lightly pushed me backward until I was laying flat on the back seat and then he climbed on top of me, inside the car. And he raped me.

He liked what he was doing to me. I was probably not the first child this crotchety old man had raped.

I didn't look older for my age. I looked like a 10 year old little girl. There was no mistaking my age at 10. I was only a baby. He knew I was only a little kid and he wanted to rape me. And he did rape me. Oh oh oh yeah. :(

Both places my dad took me to that night were strip clubs.

Let me make this perfectly clear...

The strip club didn't sex traffick me; my dad and his friend did. The strip clubs had no idea what was going on. The strip clubs were not responsible for my rape; rather, my dad, his friend and the old crotchety man were responsible for my rape.

When I turned 18, on my birthday, I auditioned at the first strip club, the one where the man didn't rape me but rather yelled at my dad.

I worked there for long enough to know there was absolutely no sex trafficking going on. Back then, we just called it rape for money/drugs. There was no terminology for what happened to us as kids. Sex trafficking wasn't a term that really existed then. There were no children being sold for sexual slavery at the strip club. There were no adults being sold to rapists. There were adults, my age and older, dancing their asses off, literally, to pay their rent and take care of their lives. There was no abuse happening at this strip club.

Shortly after, I auditioned and started dancing at the other strip club; the one where I was raped in the parking lot when I was only 10. They may have been a "sketchy" kind of place...but they also were not sex trafficking any children or adults. They were not sex trafficking strippers. They were not responsible for the old man who raped me in their parking lot when I was only 10.

Strippers were not responsible for my childhood rape/sex trafficking either.

My dad, my regular rapist and the crotchety old man were responsible that night for my rape/sex trafficking in their parking lot.Two men, desperate for substances, thought it was ok to use my little body to get what they wanted.

My dad also rape/sex trafficked me to men at Monzos Palace, Four Points Sheraton and the Holiday Inn. There were a few hunting trips I raped/ sex trafficked at. Only the men didn't hunt -- they drank, used substances and raped me. I was sex trafficked at the mechanics garage up the street, that was "Uncle Buds" place. I was sex trafficked in basements of my rapists, bedrooms of my rapists and in my own home. The locations/hotel owners/business owners did not sex traffick me.

My dad sex trafficked me.
Grown men who raped me, sex trafficked me.

If we are going to protect children, it is time to correct the narrative around child sex trafficking and child sexual abuse.

Sex trafficking and sex work are not the same.

Sex trafficking is rape.

Prostitution is an adult career. Full service sex work aka prostitution is not sex trafficking. The two don't even belong in the same category.

Sex trafficking is a form of rape.

Prostitution requires consent and is a career open only to adults.

Stripping, cam workers and other forms of erotic labor known as sex work is not sex trafficking.

Sex trafficking is a form of rape.

It's time to end conflation between sex work and sex trafficking.

Ending conflation is one of the quickest ways to end sex trafficking.

I **was not** sex trafficked because strip clubs existed. I **was not** sex trafficked because grown ass strippers were turning on grown ass men.

I was not sex trafficked because hotels existed. I was not sex trafficked because cars existed. I was not sex trafficked because beds existed. I was not sex trafficked because parking lots existed. I was not sex trafficked because hunting cabins existed. I was not sex trafficked because money existed.

I was rape/sex trafficked because my dad sex trafficked me. I was sex trafficked because there were plenty of adult men who were willing to and did rape me when I was only a child.

I was sex trafficked because grown men think it's ok to rape women and children.

Strip clubs didn't sex traffick me. My dad did.
Hotels didn't sex traffick me. My dad did.

My dad sex trafficked me.
My dad sex trafficked me.
My dad sex trafficked me.

Grown men raped me & sex trafficked me.
Grown men raped me & sex trafficked me.
Grown men raped me & sex trafficked me.

Strippers and hotels were not responsible for my childhood sex trafficking abuse.

It's time to switch the narrative, if we really want to protect children.

GROWN MEN WHO PAY to RAPE CHILDREN are SEX TRAF-FICKERS.

GROWN MEN who sex traffick are responsible for sex trafficking, not the hotel, not cars, not strippers, not hookers.

Grown
Ass
Child Rapists
RAPE/SEX TRAFFICKER MEN
are responsible for my sex trafficking abuse.

Now that we've assigned blame directly to my childhood abusers, let's look at why the current narrative around sex trafficking is to sue hotels and businesses that have nothing to do with sex trafficking.

Why do some folks fall back to the "hotel is responsible" narrative?

1. It distracts from the men who are raping children.

2. Hotels have money and want to settle quickly and quietly so their brand doesn't get destroyed.

3. FOSTA/SESTA has created an atmosphere where not only can you sue the hotel, but you are encouraged to sue the hotel. -sigh- (FOSTA/SESTA is legislation that

was passed on April 11, 2018 that harmed sex traffick
ing victims and punished prostitutes.)

4. The biggest reason - the anti-trafficking movement is
encouraging sex trafficking victims to sue the

businesses into compliance to punish prostitutes and clients of
prostitutes. Hotels are being coerced via lawsuits to comply with
the anti-trafficking movements propaganda in hope that a best
practices defense will help during settlements with victims. If
they can show that they trained employees to stop sex trafficking
(and prostitution), then maybe the lawsuits will end.

There is BIG money in anti-trafficking.

Unfortunately, the year I started to write this is the 30 year anni-
versary of my dads murder. It will be 30 years since my first sex
trafficker paid for what he did to me.

In 30 years, what happened to me as a little girl was given a name
"sex trafficking." I'm not sure why rape trafficking wasn't picked,
but I'm sure it has something to do with misogyny, our rape culture and the multi-billion dollar anti-trafficking movement.

In 30 years, all the anti-trafficking movement seemed to accom-
plish was come up with a name for what happened to me, "sex
trafficking," and encourage survivors to sue hotels, who likely
had nothing to do with their rape trafficking abuse, and collect
money for "resources". Resources is intentionally in quotes because no actual resources exist beyond the anti-trafficking organizations in house, self-made, programs that were created without
sex trafficking experts. These programs teach children how not to
be prostitutes instead of how to heal from their rape trafficking
abuse. This isn't a resource.

The anti-trafficking movement has achieved little in ending or
preventing rape/sex trafficking.

It's my opinion that sex trafficking is not even an accurate title. Sex is something that should be shared with whomever you wish, as long as all parties are consenting adults. Sex is fun. Sex is spiritual. Sex is a part of us. Sex requires consent.

Rape trafficking is more accurate of a description of what happened to me. I was raped by grown men. There was no sex involved. I was 10.
I was RAPE TRAFFICKED.

I was not a 10 year old prostitute. I was a child who was rape trafficked.

The misogynistic narrative around sex trafficking is victim blaming. Most anti-trafficking organizations manipulate victim's realities to fit their organizational grant chasing needs. They identify child rape trafficking victims as child prostitutes. They are inherently harmful to survivors.

There is BIG money in anti-trafficking.
During the COVID-19 Pandemic, MILLIONS of dollars were raised by the anti-trafficking movement for emergency COVID-19 support. Unfortunately, nearly none of this money raised went to sex trafficking victims/survivors themselves. Instead, anti-trafficking organizations have fancy new offices and "drop in centers" that only ever get visitors if they are court ordered to be there or otherwise coerced by law enforcement via a diversion program. MILLIONS raised for us and not given to us.

Sex trafficking survivors are currently struggling to survive during the pandemic.

We have no resources. We have no access to survival.

Right now, as I write this, sex trafficking survivors are in need of safe housing, food, medical care, mental health care, and child care. We have basic needs to survive that are going unmet. As sex trafficking victims/survivors, we have no access to the funds raised for us.

We are left to struggle while anti-trafficking organizations bring in millions to aid us.

Where are our resources?

'Resources' seems to be just a word and an endless circle of chasing resources, because nobody actually has real resources for sex trafficking victims and survivors.

There is BIG money in anti-trafficking, for anti-trafficking leaders and orgs.

In fact, I wouldn't be surprised if **anti-trafficking is** the biggest growing industry of today.

Unfortunately, there is little support available for sex trafficking victims or survivors ourselves. The anti-trafficking movement is gatekeeping them from us.

Oftentimes, "help" comes with strings to align your life to their morals. Many religious organizations push that the love of Jesus will save you from trafficking. They teach programs that concentrate on how not to be a hooker by bringing Jesus into our lives.

UM WHAT?

Victim blaming religious folks need to stop centering themselves. I wasn't trafficked because I didn't love Jesus enough.

I was rape trafficked because my dad trafficked me. Jesus didn't have a thing to do with it.

Telling kids that "Jesus will save you," at a time when they are being raped and abused, is not helpful. It is my opinion this is a religious form of abuse.

The anti-trafficking movement does this often.

When I was a little kid, I would pray so hard. I would get on my knees and make sure my prayer hands were exactly how Gram showed me. I was so good at my prayer hands. My fingers would all line up exactly. I would be sitting up tall, on my knees and bowing my head. Most times, I would close my eyes. I was doing it right, but Jesus wasn't listening to my prayers.

I would pray to Jesus for the bleeding to stop and when it eventually did, I thought Jesus saved me...until I got raped again and the bleeding came back.

Jesus didn't save me.

The person who murdered my dad saved me.

In over 30 years since the beginning of my abuse, the anti-trafficking movement hasn't saved any more 10 year old little girls than it did back then. Their narrative was created to go after funding and put morally unacceptable women and girls in our place. We call them misogynistic 'grant-chasers'.

The anti-trafficking movement will have you believe there is only one form of sex trafficking:
The lovestruck runaway teen who runs to be with her 'boyfriend' who isn't a boyfriend but a trafficker.

Does this happen?
Yes, absolutely; it does.

When I was a teen, this happened to me.
Survivors who experienced this form of sex trafficking are valid. However, this is the minority of children who are being sex trafficked.

We are missing the vast majority of sex trafficking victims, some as young as days old, who are being raped and/or rape trafficked by their dad, mom, uncles, "uncles" and other child pedophiles and child rapists.

We are missing the vast majority of sex trafficking happening within our broken foster system.

The anti-trafficking narrative about teenage rape/sex trafficking victims is harming teenagers and younger children alike. I'll share more on my teenage abuse in Special Kinda Broken part 2.

Our kids do not have adequate access to resources. Our society gate keeps resources from children. Our society gate keeps children's survival.

Our kids have a lack of accurate education about sex and consent.

Society is good at pushing "no means no.".

They forgot to expand.

Consent Basics:
No means no.
Maybe means no.
Yes can change to no at any second and needs to be respected immediately, if not sooner.
Yes means yes.

And don't fucking sex traffick people.

Is anyone telling boys what sex trafficking is and that you're not suppose to sex traffick another so you can survive?

Is anyone telling children it's not ok that they are a 10 year old "dancer" for parties where they are being raped by grown men?

Is anyone telling 10 year olds what rape is?

Are children being educated or are they just being pushed by the same anti-trafficking propaganda that hasn't helped 10 year old little girls end their abuse in over 30 years?

We also need to tell people, "DO NOT RAPE."

We can talk about sexual abuse being wrong and harmful all we want. But we will never end a generational rape culture until we start telling boys, "Do Not Rape. Rape is wrong. Rape is harmful. Do not sex traffick. Sex trafficking is wrong. Sex trafficking is a form of rape. We don't rape." Tell boys this when they are little. A teenager was the first person to sexually abuse me. I was 6 years old at the time. He was only a kid. But he was wrong; yes, absolutely. He abused me.

Who, exactly, told him that you don't put your fingers inside 6 year olds? Did he even know it was wrong? Did he know how harmful his actions were to me? Was he also abused?

Children are never too young to learn about rape, sexual abuse and sex trafficking. Children are always too young to experience rape, sexual abuse and sex trafficking.

Children are never too young to learn how not to sexually abuse or sex traffick others. Children are never too young to learn how not to become a rapist.

Children are never too young to learn how to protect themselves from abuse.

Ask your children, "What do you think rape is? What do you think it means to be raped? What do you do if you are raped? How can you improve your safety and protect yourself from rape?"

Start talking to your children. You cannot protect them from abuse if they don't even know the abuse exists until after they've experienced it. You cannot protect them from becoming abusers if you don't tell them how to not abuse. You cannot raise your children to not be a rapist if they don't understand what rape is.

Start talking to your children.
Start protecting your children.

They are never too young to learn how to protect themselves from abuse.

Oh Oh Oh Yeah

Oh Oh Oh Yeah
It rings through my head

Oh Oh Oh Yeah
Four words make me wish I was dead

Oh Oh Oh Yeah
He said before he raped me

Oh Oh Oh Yeah
The pain he caused he wanted to see

Oh Oh Oh Yeah
This man was sick in the head

Oh Oh Oh Yeah
To this day, his words still haunt my bed

Oh Oh Oh Yeah
Late at night I wake with a shiver

Oh Oh Oh Yeah
My life always hangs on by a thin sliver

Oh Oh Oh Yeah
He knew what he was doing to me

Oh Oh Oh Yeah
He broke my with with a maniacal glee

Oh Oh Oh Yeah
He took whatever he wanted

Oh Oh Oh Yeah
My innocence he has hunted

Chapter Four Summary

It's time to center childhood sex trafficking survivors to end child sex trafficking abuse. Stop listening to propaganda of the anti-trafficking movement.

Listen to and center lived experiences.

Hotels were not responsible for my sex trafficking abuse.

Sex workers were not responsible for my childhood sex trafficking. In all of my abuse, prostitutes and strippers were never responsible. Clients of prostitutes and strippers were never responsible for my sex trafficking rape.

My dad was responsible for my sex trafficking abuse. Grown men who raped me when I was only 9 & 10 years old were responsible for my rape trafficking abuse.

Cookies Crumble

Come and have a seat with me
Only then will you see
Our lives must be set free
Keep swallowing that glee
It won't hurt, take a knee
Evil that is carefree
Sensing his touching spree

Cruel and clear to little she
Ruin of her young life it will be
Uttered for support she did plea
Masters retort didn't agree
Bitch left, she surely did flee
Lightning drawn to a lone tree
Excruciatingly painful times for little me

COOKIES CRUMBLE

This is a long read. 5,000 words.

This chapter includes graphic details of a very violent attack I survived when I was only 10.

There is an extra *TW* (trauma warning) for this chapter.

Remember, self care is important and necessary when healing. You are important and deserve love and kindness. Take care of yourself. Take a bath. Take a walk. Take a break. Take a nap. Whatever you do, always remember to take care of yourself , too.

T ossing and turning, my little mind would not let me rest. Maybe it was too much sugar from the Christmas cookie mixing earlier; I kept sticking my finger in the batter and licking it off. Mom let me;she even encouraged it. I had never made cookies before, let alone Christmas cookies. Let alone Christmas cookies with my biological mom. Maybe that's why I couldn't sleep well.

Maybe it was "uncle Bud" who had passed out in the living room.

I heard my door open. The house was an old gas station that my grandfather had turned into a home. It was built into a small hill and was dark and dingy. Everything in that place creaked and cracked.

I could smell "uncle Bud" as he guided my dog out. The click click click of my guard dog's paw nails as he was led out of my room signaled what was to come next.

Bear, my guard dog, a full blood Rottweiler, was trained to protect me. He was trained to attack intruders.

However, I was not allowed to use any of Bear's commands on dad's friends, though. Bear was not allowed to protect me from them.

I pulled the blanket over my head and pressed play on my little pink cassette player. I knew what was to come.

The door creaked open again.

George Thorogood sang about all his ex's who lived in Texas. I wanted to grow up and go to Texas. *Maybe I would be ok there,* I thought. The more I was abused, the more I cut myself to feel better. I would physically feel better when the wound healed. The more I was abused, the more I withdrew from life and became fascinated with self-harm practices.

I created this world in my mind to escape during the abuse.

My "escape place" looked exactly like my bathroom. Yes, my bathroom was my safe space during the abuse. I'd soak in the tub and cut myself with rusty, old razor blades. It would take the pain away -- the real pain I was experiencing. **For some reason, the pain that would last a lifetime was somehow dulled when I cut myself.** It would make me stronger so I could survive. In my mind, I recreated my bathroom and I tried to escape there each time I was raped by a grown man.

Waiting was the worst with "uncle" Bud. I knew it was coming. When was sometimes hard to determine.

Sometimes, "uncle" Bud would pass out and not come into my room. That was my hope that night; he seemed to be taking too long to put Bear outside. I closed my eyes and tried to calm my little mind down.

I'll be ok. I'm a woman now and this is what women do. I'll be ok. I'll become stronger so I can be a woman. I'll be ok, I tried to convince myself.

Sadly, neither my mind nor my body was granted any reprieve that night.

"Uncle" bud had been so messed up, he couldn't even stand or walk. He crawled into my room. He actually crawled into my room to rape me.

When he couldn't crawl anymore, he collapsed on the floor, his feet still in the hallway.

Oh good; I'm safe. He fell asleep again, I thought.

Sometimes, he would pass out before, during, or after raping me. That night, I was hoping he'd pass out before he hurt me.

He couldn't walk so I was probably going to be ok if I was really quiet. I pulled the covers a little higher and tucked them in behind my head. I tried to sleep with "uncle" Bud passed out on the floor at the bottom of my bed.

I rewound the George Thorogood tape, pressed play and closed my eyes. Eventually, I drifted off to sleep.

Suddenly, I felt myself sliding down my water bed. The water was sloshing, and my legs, and bottom and back scraped the wooden frame at the foot of the bed as "uncle" Bud dragged me out of bed by my ankles and feet. He pulled me to the floor with one final tug and my head hit the bottom wood part of the water bed frame. I developed a knot on my head.

He violently raped me that night. Then he passed out on top of me, with his pants still around his ankles. His slobber ran down my cheek, to my ear, to my neck and eventually made a puddle beside my head. He finished raping me and let his semi hard penis sit inside me.

When he rolled over, I slowly and quietly tiptoed to the bathroom. I turned on the shower, got in, washed, cried and bled. I washed some more before sitting on the floor of the shower. The cold water was streaming against my broken body. I was freezing, crying and shaking . Tears were running down my face. I had a razor in hand, and of course, I started cutting. Only this time, I cut my wrists, longways.

I was only 10 years old.

I had given "uncle" Bud a hard time earlier on that day. I didn't want to send my mom away. This was my punishment. He liked it when I cried.

Earlier:

A woman came over. My dad said she was my mom and we were going to bake Christmas cookies. I had never baked cookies before. And I had never baked Christmas cookies before with a mom. I had never had a mom that didn't leave me. Maybe this one would stay. Maybe she would protect me, too. Dad left. He didn't like my new mom much; in fact, he hated her. I didn't know why she was there.

Turns out this new mom was my biological mom. The one who gave birth to me, brought me home from the hospital and walked out on me. Yeah, that mom.

Dad was a mess; substances took hold of his life. He contacted my biological mom to take care of me. Dad loved me. Even though he abused me, he loved me.

The evening started with this new mom asking me what I learned in school that day and telling me how much she missed me.

Before we got all of the cookies done, "uncle" Bud showed up. "uncle" Bud was not really my uncle. He was the mechanic from down the road who used substances. "Uncle" Bud partied with my dad.

After my dad's last girlfriend left, "uncle" Bud started coming over more. They partied a lot. Dad was heart broken. "Uncle " Bud gave drugs to my dad...so he could spend time with me.

He was one of the several "uncles" I had. Most of them sexually assaulted and raped me. Most of them gave my dad drugs and/or paid his bills to rape me. Some of them gave me ice cream money after they raped me.

Earlier that evening, "uncle" Bud plopped down on the couch. He had a needle in his hand. I sat beside him at his request. He rubbed my leg. He told me if I ever wanted to see my new mom again, I'd make her leave. He muttered a few other threats; they were devastating. " U|ncle" Bud said she was not a good person and if she stayed, he'd have to punish her and I'd never see her again.

I didn't really understand the role of a mom much. My mom walked out on me the very day she brought me home from the hospital. I ended up in the foster system until I was almost 7, when a judge thought it was best to give me to a violent man, my dad.

I knew I wanted a mom. And if this mom was killed by "uncle" Bud, I'd have to wait for the next mom to come along. I had to protect my mom. So I did.

Let's talk about Bear. Bear was my protector from everyone, except dad's friends.

Bear was a purebred Rottweiler that came from a guard dog bloodline. Dad said I was not allowed to use the special commands I learned with dad's friends or family. I was only to use them if someone broke in when my dad was out of town.

Dad would be gone for days and sometimes weeks at a time. So, Bear was supposed to be my protector.

Bear was my only friend.

It's unlikely that a child will be snatched off the street and forced into sex trafficking. It is VERY LIKELY that children are being sex trafficked by a parent/guardian/foster parent/uncle/sibling/coach/church leader etc.

I was only 9 years old when "uncle" Bud started touching me.

"Uncle Bud" was going to hurt my new mom. I did the only thing I could think to do, and that was to have Bear scare my mom.

I made Bear attack her. It was not hard, though. It was just the warning command. Bear clamped his mouth full of teeth into my mom's arm. It scared her and she left.

She didn't take me with her. She walked out as I was on the couch being sexually abused by "uncle" Bud. Eventually, I learned not to cry.

Now, as an adult, I cry all the time. Every day.

As a kid, I would cut myself more. And I would bleed more. But I would cry less. Months went by. The parties continued. Men continued to visit my room. The abuse continued. So I cut myself more and I cried less. They started stopping by when there was no party, just to visit my room. I cut more. I cried less. I spent most of the day inside my head trying to figure out a way to make the pain end while conditioning myself to not feel pain at all.

Everyone in my life had been threatened by my abusers, each on their own level with their own sick perversions. They would tell me that if I wasn't a good little girl, they would hurt my dad. When that stopped working, they told me they would kill me and when that stopped working, too, they told me they would kill my dog and make me watch them do it.

I cut more. I cried less.

This became my life.

I cut more. I cried less.

Every minute of every day, I lived in fear.

I cut more. I cried less.

I cleaned the house. I also cooked for dad because he was always in bed, not home or partying with a house full of people.

For some reason, he forgot I was a kid. I became the woman of the house. Sometimes, I wonder if he even knew I was a kid, his kid. Did he even know that I was there and hurting? Of course he did.

One of my abusers would spank me before he raped me.

I was only 9 when it started. How could a dad not see that all those free drugs and paid bills came at the cost of me?

I cut more. I cried less.

Dad knew. He always knew.

My abuse went on during the summer of 1990 until just before my dads murder on his birthday that year, six days before Christmas.

During this time period, I was sex trafficked with an 11 year old and a 6 year old.

End the conflation of prostitution (a job) and

sex trafficking (a form of rape).
Fully decriminalize sex work.

The current rhetoric is missing all the 9 year old little girls who are hurt, alone, lost, scared and want to die so the pain will end. I was filled with these feelings at age 9. The first time I tried to commit suicide, I didn't even know what suicide was. I just knew my pain needed to end.

Why aren't we saving the children?

*If you are a sex trafficking victim and you're reading this, I'd like to encourage you to hang in there. We are trying to raise our voices to raise awareness to protect you.

You are loved. ❤ [heart emoji] You are important. You don't deserve to be abused. What you're going through is not your fault. Hang on, stay strong. I love you.

WE ARE MISSING THE CHILDREN

What happened to me when I was 9-10 years old is NOT the same as prostitution. I was not a 9 year old prostitute.

What happened to me was a form of rape, by grown men, old enough to know it was wrong. This form of rape for profit is the most dehumanizing, evil form of abuse I've ever experienced.

I was raped, repeatedly, for months by adult men. They gave my dad substances and gave me ice cream money for school.

My own mom walked out on my abuse.

There were no safe spaces for me to escape my abuse.

Prostitution is NOT sex trafficking.
I was not a 9 year old prostitute.

Conflation of sex trafficking, a form of rape and prostitution, is killing both sex trafficking victims and prostitutes.

We need to end conflation of sex work and sex trafficking. Then we need to have the hard conversation that some people should not be parents or have access to children.

I was just a little girl being used, abused, and raped by grown men.

True rape/sex trafficking victims are still out there being unheard and unhelped. They lack the resources to reach out because even kids know cops don't like prostitutes . Cops identify and classify child sex trafficking victims as prostitutes instead of child rape victims. As a result, many victims don't feel safe reporting to the cops.

Victims are still out there being unheard and unhelped. The smoke and mirrors of rounding up prostitutes in the name of ending "trafficking" is allowing abusers to continue to abuse children.

Cops punish. Cops cuff.
Courts punish. Courts dictate. Courts take away freedom.

Children are getting abused. The cops and courts are not going after the real sex traffickers. The cops and courts are not fixing our broken system. The cops and courts are not providing resources such as food or emergency shelter for childhood sex trafficking victims or our youth that are at risk. The cops and courts have tried...and they have failed.

They F-A-I-L-E-D

Failed.

Dear cops & courts,

Have a seat, dig your fingers out of your ears and stick them in your mouth. It's time you stop talking and start listening.

Punishing prostitutes will NEVER END SEX TRAFFICKING. Punishing clients of prostitutes will NEVER END SEX TRAFFICKING.

You are not going to stop an abuser who wants to sex traffick 10 year old little girls by adding more laws that say, "don't abuse little girls."

We already have those laws and abusers are ignoring them. Every. Single. Day.

We have enough laws on the books in the USA to send away child-hood sex traffickers and rapists for the rest of their lives.

No matter how many laws you put on the books, nothing will change the fact that the cops and courts are not investigating, charging, ar-resting or in any way trying to go after sex traffickers.

Cops, courts and even lawmakers are targeting prostitutes and in doing so, they are mismanaging funding that is earmarked to save children from sex trafficking.

Stop targeting prostitutes.

Start targeting child rapists.

Abusers who already break the law will continue to abuse and break the law no matter how many new laws you create.

Abusers don't care about laws.

Abusers know the cops will arrest a victim and charge that victim with prostitution before arresting a rapist/sex trafficker of chil-dren (or adults).

Childhood abusers don't say, "Oh wait, there are more laws that say 'don't rape children' so now I'll behave and stop raping chil-dren."

That's. Not. How. Abusers. Work.

To save current 9-10 year old child sex trafficking victims, you must first listen to childhood sex trafficking survivors. We have lived experiences.

Childhood sex trafficking survivors are the experts and the key to end child sex trafficking.

Why is our system gatekeeping survival resources from children?

Why is the anti-trafficking movement not providing funding and resources to victims and survivors?

Nobody was responsible FOR me.
Nobody was responsible TO me.

My choices were:

- put up with abuse at home;
- group home/juvie;
- struggle & starve, alone.

I was a burden to the courts.
I was a burden to my family.
I was only 12 years old the first time I was houseless, and alone.

Put up with abuse at home;
Group Home/Juvie;
Struggle and starve, alone.

Do you want to end childhood sex trafficking?

Good.

Do you want to end youth trading sexual services to survive? Good.

So do I. Nobody should endure the abuse I did as a child.

FIRST - To end sex trafficking, we must fully decriminalize

prostitution and related offenses and end conflation of prostitution and sex trafficking.

Sex trafficking is a form of rape.

Prostitution is a service- based career.

When we decriminalize prostitution:

❤ Victims can walk into the police station and report their abusers (including traffickers) without threats of being arrested themselves.

- On many occasions, police disregard the abuse claim and/or punish the victim by arresting them. This allows abusers to go un-investigated and never held responsible for their abuse. They are free to abuse again another day.

❤ Victims can seek justice against their abusers if they decide to.

- Abusers are not being charged. Victims are being punished because they are "bad whores". Abusers are left to abuse another day; so they can abuse another victim. Pennsylvania even has a "bad whore" law that allows past sexual behavior of a rape victim to be considered to show that the victim has sex so the victim could not have possibly been raped.

❤ Those victimized by cops can seek justice and protection.

- Cops are responsible for a lot of spousal abuse. Cops are also responsible for a lot of full service sex worker abuse. There are so many cop abuses -- from rape, to physical violence, to threats of arrest, to extortion to sex trafficking, to murder and so many other abuses that take place at the hands of cops in the sex worker community.

Second - national end conflation law. Ending the conflation of sex trafficking, a form of rape, and sex work, a career, is paramount to ending sex trafficking. All funding would be diverted away from targeting prostitutes and concentrated on protecting sex trafficking victims.

Third - amnesty for sex trafficking victims and sex workers. Neither victim or sex worker can report to the cops without threat of arrest.

When we have full decriminalization of prostitution, an end conflation law and amnesty, workers and victims will then have rights, resources, and protections under the law, to exit their abuse, seek their desired form of healing and thrive in life.

Cops decide who is a prostitute or victim, taking away all self-agency of potential sex trafficking victims. This is abuse against sex trafficking victims.

What other crime victims do we arrest as a way to "save" them?

It's been over 30 years since my childhood sex trafficking abuse started. In over 30 years, the cops, courts, carceral system and the anti-trafficking movement have not come close to helping 9 year olds that are being traded by their fathers for substances.

It's over 30 years later and they are still using harmful and dehumanizing terminology such as "child prostitute." Why?

It's over 30 years later and they are not saving the children.

Cops, courts and the carceral system have had their chance to end childhood sex trafficking.

They failed. In many cases, they've made it worse.

Sex trafficking victims pay the price for their failures.

It's time to defund cops and redistribute those resources to the community. It's time to spend anti-trafficking funding ending sex trafficking instead of targeting prostitutes.

Cops, courts, and the carceral system all need to sit down while we do damage control and start to heal.

Cops should not be the gatekeepers of the survival of sex trafficking victims. Cops are arresting victims.

It's time to center voices with lived experiences.

I'm a childhood sex trafficking survivor. My dad started trading me to grown men in exchange for substances and bill payment when I was only 9 years old.

STOP taking away our rights, resources, and protection. STOP taking away our voice.

It's time to stop targeting adult full service sex workers (aka prostitutes, providers, escorts) and provide safe spaces for children and adults who are actually experiencing sex trafficking, which is a horrible form or rape. It's time to redirect arrest resources to sex trafficking victims and survivors themselves.

There is a better way to help our houseless youth population before they feel they need to trade sex to put a roof over their head or a sandwich in their belly.

Instead of funding cops,
Invest in Community.

Community partners can create **safe spaces** for childhood and adult sex trafficking survivors.

Allow youth the same, or more, resources as adults receive: Housing, food, transportation, medical care, emergency shelter, education, childcare, and more. We need to build safe spaces where our youth can have their needs met without repercussions under the law.

*Safe Spaces do NOT include cops, cuffs, courts, criminalization or control.

❤ Safe Spaces DO include love.

❤ Safe Spaces DO include education.

❤ Safe Spaces DO include food.

❤ Safe Spaces DO include safety.

❤ Safe Spaces DO include transportation.

❤ Safe Spaces DO include emergency shelter.

❤ Safe Spaces DO include housing.

❤ Safe Spaces DO include medical care.

❤ Safe Spaces DO include mental health care.

❤ Safe Spaces DO include life skills.

❤ Safe Spaces DO include listening.

❤ Safe Spaces DO include hearing.

❤ Safe Spaces DO include self-care.

❤ Safe Spaces DO include privacy.

❤ Safe Spaces DO include *cash.*

If you are not ready to meet the youth where they are, maybe you are doing it wrong. Maybe you are causing further harm instead of helping.

Cuffing kids is not helping. Criminalizing kids is not helping.

They are young .
They are not without a mind of their own.

Many kids want to run away.

Some do run away.

Some kids don't have a reason to run away.
But many do have a reason to run away.

Some ran away to the backyard at 5 years old because they didn't get mac-n-cheese for dinner.

Some at 15 because daddy wouldn't stop touching their private parts.

Why aren't we talking about this?

Cops abuse kids, too. They aren't a safe space for child sex trafficking victims.

My question would be, how many victims have been sexually assaulted and/or raped by cops during the "saving" process? How many were under 18? Under 21? Under 25? How many cops are preying on young prostitutes because our laws allow them to manipulate and use barbaric practices during arrest?

How to end Human Trafficking:

> Step One - full decriminalization of prostitution and related crimes. End conflation of prostitution and sex trafficking. Amnesty when reporting violent crimes.

Step Two - create Safe Spaces full of resources for both youth and adults. Offer resources to victims/survivors of sex trafficking AND to prostitutes AND youth. Stop gatekeeping resources.

Listen to Sex Workers who are survivors.

Ask your lawmakers to put an end conflation of prostitution and rape trafficking. Ask them to support: 1. Amnesty 2. End Conflation 3. Full Decriminalization

The children are waiting.

Chapter Five Summary

End the conflation of prostitution and sex trafficking. I not a child prostitute. There is no such thing as a child prostitute. This harmful rhetoric is talking over victims. It is not allowing space for the conversation we should be having, not everyone should be a parent and not everyone should have access to children.

Conflation is killing children. This language is harmful to child sex trafficking victims and survivors. The anti-trafficking movement is morphing their terminology again to keep their money train going. Don't let them erase child sex trafficking victims and survivors.

Phone Calls, Trials and Zoos...Oh My

Scared and shattered
Torn and tattered

Not knowing who to trust
My insides ready to bust

Pushed to defend her on the stand
Most of my testimony they canned

They didn't want the world to see
What he was really doing to me

Darkness stained my young heart
Forever tearing my world apart

Men visited my bed at night
They filled me with so much fright

Nobody cared or wanted to find out
They didn't want to create any doubt

They had a job to get done
For a grieving mother's son

For a life ended and someone must pay
They didn't give a fuck about me that day

They didn't care what damage they did
They didn't care I was only a little kid

They didn't think of my forever pain
They didn't think they'd push me insane

Pushing a young child on the stand
Not knowing where their testimony will land

It's a risky chance they take

Exposing the lies and the true snake

They wanted a win
They didn't want to uncover his sin

They didn't care the cost
They didn't care my life was lost

My abuser was dead as could be
Protected by his death was a young little me

PHONE CALLS, TRIALS AND ZOOS...OH MY

For most of my life, I thought I killed my dad.

I know I didn't pull the trigger.I wasn't even in the same state when the trigger was pulled.

When I was a kid, I thought I was the one who set off the final chapter in my dad's life, though.

I was only 10 years old.

The shower was where I cut myself to learn how to cry less. The shower was also where I naired, because I was a "woman now." The shower was where I sat and shook until the water ran cold. The shower was where I bled and tended my wounds. The shower was my only safe space in the world -- the place where I wanted to die.

The shower was where I figured out how to save my own life, before I tried to end my own life, again.

It was Christmas time in 1990.

There were no decorations in my house that year. The only jolly festivities were the now occasional party. Parties slowed down once dad started dating again.

I was getting raped less.

There were less parties.
Less visitors stopped by to abuse me.

However, I was home alone quite a lot.
I ate cream of wheat for 2 weeks straight, for both breakfast and dinner. I was lucky I had the free lunch card at school. Although embarrassing as a kid, I'm glad I ate.

My dog was the only company I had. Bear was my buddy and my protector. Bear was permitted to be my personal weapon for strangers.

I was warned to never use Bear on my dad's friends, though.

Bear was a purebred Rottweiler, trained to attack. Trained to obey my dad and me. I was strictly forbidden to use bear on anyone we knew. Only strangers.

Dad started dating strippers and getting his substances from them. He would go out with them all the time and leave me home with Bear.

To those strippers, some of whom I danced with when I turned 18, thank you for being you. Unknown to you, you provided a respite in my abuse because you just gave my dad substances and money, expecting nothing in return. Thank you for supporting my dad's substance use. The ripple effects of your kindness reached me when I was only 10. Your actions are what harm reduction looks like. Keep that shit up. Thank you, strippers, for saving little me.

I was 10 when the phone rang…
I was ready…I came up with the plan in the shower…

Over and over again, I practiced.

My plan was ready. I knew she would call soon. I knew she would protect me.

I spent too much time in the shower. Cutting. Crying. Learning how not to cry. Hurting. Ready to die. This was no existence for a

10 year old.

Kids at school were getting dressed up and talking about the presents that Santa was going to bring while I sat in the tub, letting the shower run cold, trying to figure out how not to die. I was trying to talk myself out of killing myself before I even knew the term 'suicide' existed.

I was ready to be saved...

She called.

I desperately needed somebody to save me.

"Uncle" Bud and my other uncles were hurting me. Dad was still beating me, only more now. He started hitting me in the face, open handed. He would sit on my feet and wail on me with his belt. He would backhand me if I didn't make his sliced fried potatoes just right. I still can't eat sliced fried potatoes without it being a trigger of my childhood abuse. He backhanded me, the potatoes would go flying and then I would have to clean up and then make new potatoes. If the new ones were good, I would only get 5 lashes with the belt. If they were bad, I'd get more.

Dad would give me to his friends, so they could rape me. I hurt. I was broken. I wanted it all to end.

She was going to save me.

I knew she would.

I wanted to go live with her.

She called. My dad wasn't home. I cried. She promised me I would be ok. She said she loved me and missed me. I missed her, too. I wanted her. I needed her to protect me. I needed her to save me.

Only, I didn't understand that the only way left to save the little 10 year old me, would be to end the life of my almost 31 year old dad.

She asked my dad to come get her and bring her home. Of course he said yes. Although he abused her, I think he loved her with all he had. He left to go get her and bring her home.

I was getting a mom back, one that protected me as much as she could.

My dad loved me. But my dad abused me.

My dad loved her. But my dad abused her.

She hung up the phone.

My dad packed a bag and hit the road.

She went to the store to buy a gun.

My last words to my dad were "I hate you".

At age 10, I did hate my dad. He wouldn't let me go with him. I needed her. She would protect me.

He left me at home.

He drove.

He knocked on the door.
She called out for him to enter.

He opened the door.
She shot him.
She killed him.

She saved me the only way she knew how to end the abuse that came with my dad. She saved her life that day and mine, too.

I don't even know if she knew my dad was sex trafficking me.

She went to jail.
She was a victim punished for her survival.

I went to live with my pap.
Pap abused me, too.
Pap got rid of my dog, my protector.

So pap could abuse me more.
Pap feared my dog.
Pap gave my dog to a business in Youngwood, PA, to be retrained as a guard dog.

He told me that Bear got run over by a car and died. He lied.

I found out shortly after my first child was born that Bear didn't die when I was a kid. Bear died when I was 19.

I lost my dad.
I lost my stepmom.
I lost my dog.
Pap was now raping me.

I was so broken.

On December 25, 1990, I learned there was no Santa. My family had forgotten to get me gifts that year. My dad's funeral was on Christmas Eve, 1990.

My family was so distraught by my dad's death and the funeral that it didn't register that my dad wasn't coming home.

When dad died, Santa died 6 days later.

I woke up to 1 gift, which my dad purchased before he died.

They forgot to tell Santa I really needed him that year.

Pap started touching me on December 20, 1990. The day after my dad died.

Pap died weeks after I finished the first draft of this book -- days before we were placed in quarantine during the 2020 Covid-19 pandemic.

I didn't attend his funeral. I didn't cry.

I ended the generational sexual abuse in my family. My pap never touched my kids. Never.

December 1990 quickly became August 1991...

THE TRAIL

I was almost 11. I was broken and being sexually abused by my pap.

My Gram was heartbroken after my dad died. No parent should outlive their children. My Gram was never the same. She said mean things about the woman who saved my life. My gram was a momma who was mourning the death of her son. My Gram was so hurt. She was so broken.

My Gram married my pap as a 15 year old child to escape her own sexual abuse at the hands of her own dad.

My Gram divorced my pap when my dad was still a kid.

Even though my dad had an evil side to him, he was my Grams son, so she loved him. I loved him, too. He was my dad. Of course I loved him.

We arrived for the trial. The prosecutor's office sent a personal guide to drive us around, and make sure we got to court. The guide drove us to the spot where my dad was murdered and took us to the market in Tijuana.

When folks were asking me questions about what happened, I tried to tell them about the men raping me.
"Where did they hurt you?" they asked and just as quickly as they asked, they hushed me up when I pointed to my private regions. People hurt my privates and they didn't care. My pap told our personal guide that I was confused due to the murder of my dad.

My pap was raping me. Our personal guide assigned for the the prosecution, assisted my pap and silenced my rape and sex trafficking abuse that day. The prosecution didn't protect me. They protected their "win".

They then scared me and threatened me with jail time if I lied on the stand.

They threatened a 10 year old little girl with jail time. Wow.

"You know if you lie on the stand, they can put you in jail. You need proof or it's a lie." They manipulated me and scared me. The proof parts have always stuck with me..."you need proof or it's a lie."

I got on the stand, did the bible thing and told the truth. Exactly as they scared me into doing.

As an adult looking back, I think the prosecution side was so worried about keeping my rapes hidden that they missed the one thing that changed the charges from murder to involuntary manslaughter.

I told them about my dad trying to cut off my fingers. On the stand. Under oath. When I was only 10 years old.

After I testified, our guide suggested we go to the Zoo, since I've had such a hard day.

I wasn't confused.
I was abused.

They threatened 10 year old me with jail time because my sexual abuse wouldn't fit their case and then bribed me to hush up about the sexual abuse that happened by sending me to the fucking zoo.

My family had said my dad just physically disciplined me. When they put me on the stand, they stopped asking questions after I told them that my dad tried to cut off my fingers and my stepmom stopped him. I still had a small scar on my pointer finger back then. She took a beating for trying to save my fingers that day. Her medical records from that day (and others) were present in the courtroom.

They didn't uncover most of the abuse in court. Broken bones, black eyes, belts and knives. The abuse, the guns, the violence...

They came nowhere near the sexual abuse and sex trafficking rape of me BY MY dad, their "victim."

Their "victim" was my abuser. He was my first sex trafficker.

The state said my dad was a victim.

No, my dad never sexually touched me himself. He only benefited by trading me for substances and money to his adult friends to rape me, as a little kid.

The prosecution wanted a win. The prosecution didn't care at what cost that win would come .

Their win came at the cost of me.

The prosecution silenced me.
The prosecution put the woman I wanted to live with in jail.

The prosecution didn't protect me.

The prosecution wanted a win more than they wanted to protect a 10 year old little girl who was a sex trafficking victim.

Testifying in court was a traumatic experience for me.

I thought my stepmom was going to take me home and continue to protect me and love me and be my new mom again.

My saviors charges were lessened from 1st degree murder to involuntary manslaughter. They sent her to prison.

The judge said some pretty crappy things about the woman who saved my life. His opinion was misguided. My dad wasn't the victim; my dad was the abuser.

After the trial, I was supposed to go live at Grams. My Gram was so upset with me after I testified that she didn't want me to live with her anymore. She left me with my pap, who she knew sexually abused my aunt as a child. My Gram stopped calling me her pickle that year. It wasn't until I was a young adult that she picked it back up. Every time she called me pickle, I looked at my little one and promised myself to protect them and never let them experience the abuse I did as a child.

My gram broke my heart and punished me. My punishment was to live with my known rapist grandfather.

My Gram punished me because I told the truth about her son who abused me, under oath, as I was threatened into doing.

Later in life, Gram and I became close. On her death bed, she apologized for everything and admitted she thought my dad was raping me right before he died.

I didn't have the heart to tell her what her son did to me.

I told her, "No Gram; dad never raped me." I didn't lie...I didn't tell the entire truth either.

She knew. She always knew.

She made right by me and protected me and my young ones until she died. She helped me untangle the abuse I experienced as a teenager. She eventually embraced my career as a stripper and hooker. She was very close to my kids.

My Gram did wrong by me when I was a kid. Honestly, I'm not sure she knew any other way. My Gram was also abused by my Pap when she was only a kid. She was his child bride.

I miss my Gram.
I need her now more than ever.

Are we re-traumatizing children for our own personal/ professional purposes or for pennies or power?

The court system had a chance to help me and they failed. Instead of providing support and resources, the court re-traumatized me and tokenized me to get their "win."

I was only 10 years old.

She saved my life. She was my only real protector. They sent her to prison. They got their "win" and sent a hero to prison.

She ended the sex trafficking abuse that I was experiencing; whether she knew of the abuse or not, I don't know.

She saved me that day, however.

Nobody listened to me. Nobody talked to me beyond lawyers and staff coaching me on what to say while simultaneously silencing the sex trafficking rape abuse I suffered.

The judge and prosecutors office re-traumatized me, so they could get a win in court.

They GOT a BIG WIN.

They punished me, a victim, who was abused by my dad while sentencing a 10 year old child to many more years of sexual, physical, mental, psychological and emotional abuse.

Big win, for who, exactly?

The court/prosecutor's office offered no resources to me. They traumatized a 10 year old and then offered nothing for me to be ok. No counseling, no meditation therapy, no art therapy, no form of support whatsoever.

The judge and prosecutors office put their professional record above the safety of a child. The DA & prosecuters office tokenized me, the daughter and victim of a murdered **sex trafficker,** for their WIN.

They protected my abuser to get their win.

The court re-traumatized me.
There were no reparations to seek mental health care for their hidden abuses. No resources list. No actual way for me to heal or be ok existed. The court system didn't care about my well being. They don't care what harm they do to victims. Their only goal is to get that win!

Catholic Charities (Greensburg, PA) re-traumatized me as a kid.
I see things very black and white. Grey is a difficult area for me. I am autistic. When the woman at Catholic Charities asked me why I wasn't "behaving" for my grandparents, I told them. More on this in the next chapter.

My Gram broke my heart when I was 10. How could she be so hurt and broken that she punished a child by sending them to live with a known child rapist?

My pap was abusing me, my dad was just murdered, of course I was going to act out.

My Gram. My Gram re-traumatized me.
She was tough on me. She taught me valuable life lessons. She helped me when my little one was born. My Gram was at the hospital during my child's birth. She told me that I am the one who holds the power to break the sexual abuse cycle in our family. The abuse cycle that she was too weak herself to break. She shared where she failed and helped me navigate how to protect my little one. She was an amazing Gram to a very broken adult grandchild. She made things right with me in her own way. She tried to make up for what she did when I was a kid.

I forgave her long ago.

I miss her. I need her. Right now.

My Gram always said I was a special kinda broken and that God loved me extra because of it.

I don't know about the God part...but...

I am a special kinda broken.
I'll never be ok, and that's perfectly ok.

Be careful not to re-traumatize victims/survivors. Your case, career, cash, comfort and cookies are not to be centered above survivor care, concern and well-being.

Never re-traumatize child sex trafficking survivors. Never re-traumatize adult sex trafficking survivors. Never re-traumatize.

Chapter Six Summary

Are we re-traumatizing children for our own personal/professional purposes or for pennies or power?

Be extra careful not to re-traumatize survivors. Your case, career, cash, comfort and cookies are not to be centered above survivor care, concern and well-being.

Never re-traumatize child sex trafficking survivors. Never re-traumatize adult sex trafficking survivors. Never re-traumatize.

Cathloic Disparities

Power and Purpose

Power has the ability to destroy even the most righteous souls.
Power goes straight to their head as they create lifelong holes.

Power held by the key holders is way above our head.
They keep us starving and barely on this side of dead.

Power is not evil, it's the holder that pulls the strings.
Power is abused, the brokenness it brings.

Power abusers are sadistic, don't you see?
They get off on hurting you and me.

Power abusers will say victims are confused
Reality is, victims are being abused.

Power abusers lay the blame at your door.
Power abusers say you are a broken chore.

Power abusers don't abuse all they know.
They look for the ones pushed out of the show.

Power abusers seek desperation and pain.
They are only here for their sick, fucked up gain.

Power abusers seek easy control.
They think little of their harmful role.

Power abusers will have us believe
We are lost and will never achieve.

Power abuser will smile in your face
While they tear apart victims and put us in our place.

Power abusers will crush your life
They will create an endless wave of strife.

Power abusers will lay fault at your door.
To them, you're nothing more than a childhood whore.

Don't believe these abusers they will lie
They want to see you suffer, they want to see you cry.

Don't believe these abusers they will scream and shout
And have you believe their will is what your life is all about.

Don't believe these abusers they will crush your will
They will encourage you to swallow that life ending pill.

Don't believe these abusers they will make you see
All of your fears, they'll never let you be.

Don't believe these abusers they will squash your dreams
They get off listening to your lifelong screams.

Center your life in all you do
There are so many who care about you.

Center you happiness and all you need
Rise above all of their greed.

Center your peace and your joy
You deserve to eat the cake as you play with your new toy.

Center yourself with love
Draw your power from up above.

Center your needs and you will soon find
There is a future, and occasionally a calm mind.

Center healing your inner spirit
What you have, they do fear it.

You'll be alright, you'll be ok
No matter what the "experts" say.

Listen, learn and explore.
Stand up straight as you walk through that door.

Love yourself and hold on tight
No matter the pain, you're gonna be alright.

Your purpose will shine true
When you give yourself permission to heal and unconditionally
show love to you.

CATHOLIC DISPARITIES

Catholic Charities saved the day for my abuser.

After my dad died, I went to live with my pap and granny. They were always so nice to me. Granny got me new school clothes one year. They always fed me, even when I wasn't hungry. My Granny was Italian and loved to cook; she always had a meal ready for me. They remembered my birthday and even got me a lot of Christmas gifts. They seemed to help dad out a lot. They cared about me. They loved me.

I was staying with them when dad left. They went bowling that night, leaving me with my aunt. When they came home, they woke me up.

They told me my dad had been murdered.

The very next day, my pap started sexually abusing me.

I was displaying behaviors that my grandparents were concerned about. Deciding counseling was the answer, they took me to Catholic Charities in Greensburg, PA.

We all talked to my counselor together, before my one on one time with her.

A few sessions in, we discussed sexual abuse. My therapist asked me if anyone had touched me in my private areas.

I told her about what my dad did to me. I also told her that my pap had been sexually abusing me since December 20, 1990.

I told her.

She said, "Don't be afraid, you can tell me," so I did.

I cried. And I waited for her to fix me. To end the abuse. To tell my pap to stop. To tell him he was hurting me.

Pap took me to my next appointment.

The therapist talked to pap alone while I sat in the waiting room.

My therapist asked me to join her and my pap.

I sat down.

The therapist explained to me that I was confused about what happened with my dad and my pap. They both claimed that such things don't happen to good little girls, and I was a good little girl. They further went on to explain that my confusion was due to the sudden loss of my dad at such a young age.

I wasn't confused.
I was abused.

My therapist was working with my rapist to manipulate me into silence. Catholic Charities abused me by covering for my rapist and gaslighting me. I wasn't fucking confused.

I was being raped and abused.

Abusers seek positions in which they can easily abuse their desired targets. This happens in families, organizations, harm reduction spaces and anywhere else abusers have easy access to abuse their perfect victim(s).

Stop saying children are confused when you really should be saying they were abused. How can I support them?

Stop protecting abusers.
Stop protecting folks with a savior complex and start listening to lived experiences.

When I started activism'ing, I was not surprised to find various levels of abusers. From exploiters, to sex traffickers, to labor traffickers, the abuse runs rampant. It's time to question who has control of victims and survivors resources and why they are not being made readily available to victims and survivors, directly. **Where is our, sex trafficking victims/survivors, funding and resources?**

Abusers are gatekeeping our resources. There are no actual resources for childhood sex trafficking victims and survivors beyond the "in house" developed programs that teach sex trafficking victims and survivors how not to be a prostitute. This is a form of child/adult abuse. It is conversion therapy, to convert abuse victims away from becoming prostitutes. None of it provides the "help" sex trafficking victims need. None of it is centered around caring for children or adults who have been raped.

They are "treating" survivors of rape abuse by teaching them a program on how not to be a prostitute.

Read that again and think about it for a second.

Have you ever experienced rape or sexual assault/abuse/harassment?

Could you imagine your rape being ended by being arrested and coerced into a prostitute conversion program?

Could you imagine the treatment for your rape was blaming you?

Child sex trafficking victims are not child prostitutes. There is no such thing as a child prostitute.

Prostitution is a career for adults only. Much like being a doctor, surgeon, lawyer, judge, or a therapist is a career for adults only.

If a child stabs another child, we don't say they were a child surgeon. Please stop identifying anyone under 18 as a child prostitute.

The anti-trafficking movement has been identifying child rape trafficking victims as child prostitutes for a long time. That needs to end, immediately.

This terminology and similar tactics are utilized to blame victims and dehumanize sex trafficking victims and survivors.

The anti-trafficking propaganda is not covering how to protect child sex trafficking victims who are 6 years old being sex trafficked, raped and abused. They don't care about the 6 year olds being abused. That won't bring in their millions.

If they have to start spending their millions on real resources, then where will they get their money for themselves?

Nothing about the anti-trafficking movement is what support or resources look like.

Abusers fill their ranks and exploit and abuse to further their own goals, with little regard to sex trafficking victims who need support.

Abusers should never be in a position to gate keep survival resources. Gatekeeping gives them all the leverage they need to abuse victims, thus further compounding the trauma.

When we are vulnerable, it becomes easier for the abuser to manipulate us. At times, abusers will seek consent to abuse us.

They will swoop in to "save us" and then place us into a group home or conversion therapy program for "morally unacceptable" women and girls.

This is not new information. The anti-trafficking movement has been morphing their terminology to suit their own selfish desires, providing the absolute minimum for victims/survivors ourselves, for decades.

Why haven't they saved the 6 year olds, 9 year olds or 11 year olds who are being raped by daddy, uncle "bud', coaches, therapists, religious leaders and other folks who have easy access to abuse children?

Abusers seek positions of power in which it is easy to abuse their desired victims.

The narrative of the anti-trafficking movement needs to change in order to protect children from rape/sex trafficking abuse. This narrative allows easy access for abusers to further abuse folks who are seeking services to heal.

Current Narrative -

Child sex trafficking victims are teenagers who fall in love with their sex trafficker.

Does this happen? Absolutely. Is it abuse? Absolutely.

We are all well aware of this specific type of sex trafficking that targets primarily teenagers and young adults as well as folks with mental health disabilities.

According to Polaris Project 2019, the data report is as follows:

Age 0-8 - 82
Age 9-11 - 46
Age 12-14 - 152
Age 15-17 - 253

Let me break all of this down:

Anti-trafficking propaganda aims to "save " runaway youth aged 15-17 for trading sexual services to fulfill their survival needs because our society gatekeeps survival resources from children. Runaway youth have no access to survival resources such as food, emergency shelter, permanent shelter, medical care and other life sustaining resources without being arrested and sent to a group home or program.

Why isn't the anti-trafficking movement lobbying Congress to provide these resources directly to runaway youth? This would have prevented my rape/sex trafficking abuse between ages 15-17. More on this in the next book.

For now, please question everything about the anti-trafficking movement.

Most anti-trafficking "rescue operations" work with police and if the teenager does not comply, they will be cuffed and criminal-ized.

None of this is what "help" looks like.

Why is our society gatekeeping resources from these children?

The anti-trafficking movement has educated society on how to identify potential youth victims aged 15-17. There were 253 victims identified in this age range.

There were also 280 youth aged 14 and younger that the anti-trafficking movement isn't educating us about. Their propaganda isn't saving any 6 year old being sex trafficked, brutally raped and abused.

According to the Polaris report, there were 82 children who were sex trafficked between age 0 to age 8. And 46 between age 9 to age 11, the category I fit into when my sex trafficking began.

Why isn't the anti-trafficking movement educating us on how to "save" the children under 14?

Maybe it's because the anti-trafficking movement doesn't care about saving the children. All they seem to care about is saving young women, girls, trans women and non binary folks from becoming a prostitute by coercing them into anti-prostitution programs.

Their data has a disclaimer at the bottom that states:

"[3]Exact age at the time the trafficking began is known for only 4% of the trafficking victims and survivors in this data set."

Hmmm, weird.

Why is the age at time sex trafficking began only known for 4% of victims and survivors?

Oh because their DATA is based on **hotline callers**, not actual sex trafficking victims.

Do we present crime stats based on 911 callers? No. That would be irresponsible and manipulative.

Then why is a hotline being permitted to manipulate the entire country by posting anti-trafficking statistics based on hotline callers?

Hotline callers, who are not sex trafficking victims themselves, but third parties such as law enforcement, probation officers and NGO's who benefit off of saving sex trafficking "victims".

This is not accurate research and is downright manipulative and disturbing. Manipulating data to fund a moralistic war against prostitutes is not real research...

It's also not saving the children.

Do you know who calls the Polaris Hotline to "save" sex trafficking victims?

1.) Police.
2.) Nosey church ladies who want prostitution to end.
3.) Community members who see a young woman who is dressed "too sexy", so they must call the police and "save" them!

Very few actual sex trafficking victims/survivors call the Polaris hotline because we do not want to be saved via cops, cuffs, coercion and conversion.

Sex trafficking survivors want the anti-trafficking movement to stop gatekeeping our resources.

Question everything about the anti-trafficking movement.

Polaris has no real resources for sex trafficking survivors beyond a referral to a lawyer to assess if anyone, like a hotel, can be sued for our sex trafficking abuse.

Hotels don't sex traffick people for renting rooms to sex trafficking rapists. How is a hotel to know they are renting to a rape/sex trafficker?

Nah, this "resource" (lawyers to sue) is just a smoke and mirrors tactic to settle out of court because the hotel doesn't want the scandal in the media.

Suing hotels will never end sex trafficking.
Suing hotels will never prevent sex trafficking.

Suing hotels will only make hotels clamp down on their rules, oftentimes creating so many barriers that sex trafficking victims cannot even rent a room to seek shelter. If a victim cannot rent a hotel room, how are they supposed to escape their abuser?

No anti-trafficking organizations are providing resources that victims/survivors need to exit their abuse, heal and thrive in life.

Pushing folks into governmental assistance is not a resource; it is a life sentence to poverty, almost impossible to escape.

There are income guidelines that remove you from all resources the second you make 1 extra dollar...as if that 1 extra dollar will magically create $200 in food resources, medical and housing.

Governmental assistance is not a resource.
Governmental assistance is a life sentence to poverty.

Where are all the actual resources?

Where are the mental health resources, beyond in house created anti-prostitution programs they develop themselves, without sex trafficking survivors or experts?

Why are rape/sex trafficking mental health experts within these programs absent?

Where are all the sliding scale mental health professionals that survivors can hire? Outside of NGO's (non governmental organizations, often times I am referring to nonprofits) who benefit off of or abuse?

WHERE IS THE 800 NUMBER HOTLINE FOR SEX TRAFFICKING VICTIMS/SURVIVORS...you know the hotline you can call for crisis support? Where is the hotline with rape/sex trafficking experts to help guide survivors through our emotional emergencies?

Oh wait, there is no such hotline or any other resources, because anti-trafficking orgs want to keep money in house, so their organization becomes more profitable.

Profits are prioritized above the care of sex trafficking victims and survivors.

Where is the housing support? Where are the cash rent grants? Vehicle grants?

Where are the millions they raised for the "emergency COVID-19 relief"?

Not one sex trafficking survivor I know has been able to access $1 dollar of the emergency COVID-19 relief. Not a single dollar.

Claiming you have resources for sex trafficking victims and survivors when you don't is a form of abuse.

Claiming you have resources when all you have is a resource list to send victims/survivors in an endless loop of "call this place or call that place to call this place again," is not a resource. It is abuse.

Keeping survivors so frustrated in their search of resources is a common tactic of the anti-trafficking movement.

Anti-trafficking organizations use our trauma porn stories so they can raise funding for their organizations, leaving little to no resources or supports available for sex trafficking victims and survivors ourselves.

Our resources and survival should be prioritized above anti-trafficking organizations who profit off of our abuse.

Anti-trafficking organizations profit off of the abuse of sex trafficking victims/survivors. Why would they ever want to end sex trafficking? If they end sex trafficking, their organizations will go out of business.

Why hasn't a single anti-trafficking organization worked on legislation to have sex trafficking victims and survivors included for disability benefits of the maximum amount permitted, not some bottom of the barrel "you never had a job" crap "so here's $783 bucks a month." MAXIMUM payments.

We will never be ok. We didn't ask to be rape trafficked as children. We don't deserve to live in utter poverty because we were broken as children. Why isn't the anti-trafficking movement working on rape/sex trafficking victims/survivors disability benefits?

There are no resources created for us yet.

At 9 years old, I was broken.

I am a special kinda broken.
I'll never be ok.
And that's ok.

In the 30+ years since the beginning of my rape/sex trafficking abuse, there are no more resources available for children to exit their abuse and seek support. There are no resources, period.

Where's our 3k/mth lifetime disability check with medical benefits, housing support and food? Where's the anti-trafficking organizations working on this legislation?

Oh wait...there are none that I can find.

Why don't academics and mental health professionals have a DSM term and definition for what happens to the brains of 9 year old little kids who are violently and brutally raped so much, for profit, that they try to take their own life?

There isn't one.

Mismanagement of anti-trafficking funding and narrative is allowing anti-trafficking organizations to withhold support and services from victims and survivors. This is abuse. This keeps children and adults in their rape/sex trafficking abuse while the anti-trafficking organizations make millions to collect their own real estate and helicopters, for themselves.

People in positions of power gatekeep our resources. This is a form of abuse. "Follow our program and we will allow you to eat" is coercion and abuse.

Why aren't we removing abusers from these spaces? Abusers seek positions of power in which it is easy for them to abuse.

Just give resources directly to rape/sex trafficking victims and survivors.

Telling our story is hard for us. Simply identifying as a rape/sex trafficking survivor is hard for us.

The ups and downs, the anger, sadness, tears and loneliness. The self blame, the self hate and the self destructive behaviors are very real. The love, the loss, the losing the love and the abuse interwoven into all of the delicate parts of who we have become; we are fragile. Be kind to us.

The inability to trust, the constant act of being on guard, never relaxing, fear around every corner, waiting for the next person to tokenize or exploit us further as they pretend to "help," takes a toll on us.

Abusers recognize my kinda brokenness. They seek it out, manipulate and abuse it.

I have been sex trafficked multiple times in my life under a variety of circumstances.

The one thing that was always in common, I couldn't report my abuser(s) safely without fear of them sending cops, cuffs, and criminalization my way.

Sex trafficking victims cannot report without fear of arrest.

The debilitating effects ripple through our work, play, rest and healing...on a daily basis.

Healing only to be abused again to heal again to be abused again to heal again to be abused again...

It is an endless cycle for some of us.

Some of us are stuck so deep into the abuse that we become easy targets for abusers. We become the perfect victims. The ones nobody would believe if we told our truth. The ones who are silenced and reminded we are a prostitute or too broken or too "crazy" to have a voice. "Nobody would believe you," we are often told.

Speaking about our abuse is harmful and healing all at once. The only support we have is each other, fellow rape/sex trafficking survivors.

Society wants us dead.
They label sex trafficking victims as prostitutes. They target, rape and abuse both sex trafficking victims and prostitutes.

When we choose, as a society, to only accept some accounts of sex trafficking rape and abuse while ignoring others that don't fit into our definition of what sex trafficking looks like, we are missing the majority of sex trafficking victims and survivors.

We are missing those 82 children ages 0-8 years young that Polaris reported on. Their "research" is based on only 4% of survivors.

If 100% of stats were reported in a similar fashion, we could be missing 2,100 children who are under age 8 and as young as minutes/days/weeks/months old. Their stats are only based on hotline callers. What about the majority of sex trafficking victims who refuse to utilize the hotline?

Where are the real statistics on sex trafficking?

How many young children are we missing while the anti-trafficking movement misuses anti-trafficking funding?

Abusers are found in counseling settings, law enforcement organizations, hospital settings, mental health settings, religious organizations, anti-trafficking organizations, harm reduction spaces and other areas where abusers have easy access to vulnerable folks.

Abusers do not live by the same moral code you may. An abusers goals are to abuse, hurt, harm, control, destroy, beat, rape, torture, kidnap, assault, kill and/or more.

Abusers each have specific types of abuse they are drawn to; their goals are to harm another human being. Harm their victim. Take the power from their victims and morph it into their own form of self power. They live for this feeling. They hunt for this feeling. They abuse to achieve this feeling. They love this feeling often more than anything else, including the right to human life.

When these abusers are in positions of power over children who have been sexually abused, the survivor often becomes re-victimised.

Many of these abusers are sadists, they love when other folks hurt and are harmed. Yes, people like this exist. They become master manipulators of their victims...

"Who would believe you? You're crazy. Your file says so."

"Maybe you're confused, that's a pretty out there story you are telling."

"Bad things don't happen to good little girls. And you're a good little girl, right?"

It's time to put the spotlight on the abusers.

It's time to stop victim blaming.
It's time to call out the pedophiles and rapists being hidden in families, medical facilities, academia, law enforcement, the car-

ceral system, religious organizations, anti-trafficking organizations, harm reduction spaces and more.

What happens to a survivor when they seek support from their counselor, who turns around and manipulates them to further abuse them?

What happens when a survivor checks into an inpatient mental health facility, with little to no family and a history of mental health difficulties? What happens if their health history lists rape or other violent sexual abuses against them? What happens when they are not mentally cognizant of the world around them? What happens when an abuser is an orderly or a nurse or a phlebotomist or security guard or a doctor or a counselor? What happens when they constantly transfer you to keep your sex trafficking abuse hidden?

What happens when a survivor reports to the police only to be targeted, harassed and wrongly labeled as a prostitute instead of a sex trafficking victim?

Oh wait...they prey on us and target survivors to re-victimize us. Because after all, who would believe the "crazy" person, right?

It's time to end the abuse and misuse of anti-trafficking funding, personnel and resources...and redistribute resources directly to sex trafficking survivors.

The anti-trafficking movement isn't even discussing the sex trafficking abuse taking place within mental health institutions.

Why is that?

Sex trafficking survivors are easy targets, because we are a special kinda broken.

Much like the abuse at Catholic Charities I experienced as a kid, many folks in mental health spaces rewrite the history of mental health patients, because after all, who would believe us? We are "crazy."

Just because the file says so, it doesn't make it true. Doctors, nurses and others can and do lie in medical files of mental health patients. We are listed as "noncompliant" or "incorrigible" and written off as troublemakers.

All. The. Time.

When some have no answers on how to fix us, they simply lie/ guess to further their mission to "help" us. Only they never really help us. They cover up abuse and then list things like "patient combative" or "patient manipulative." When the reality is they would rather quickly slap a label on us and throw some pills down our throat than to listen to us and try to support our needs.

In 2013-2017, I took a few trips to the mental health inpatient emergency facility located at the hospital. After being discharged from the Fort Walton Beach Medical Center mental health unit, a worker on the unit messaged me on a dating app. He did not disclose that he knew me from his job on the mental health inpatient unit, the week prior...until he had his hand around my throat while he violated my consent.

He told me to relax, because it'll go in easier and hurt less. He choked me harder. When I fought, he told me he saw me on the mental health unit and nobody would believe me because I'm fucking crazy, so I should just relax and enjoy myself. I was a grown woman in my 30s, being anal raped by an abuser who preyed on me while I was seeking mental health services at an inpatient facility.

Abusers seek positions in which they have easy access to their ideal victims.

When are we going to talk about sexual abuse and sex trafficking within the mental health field? Within the inpatient mental health field?

When are we going to talk about abusers who specifically seek these positions so they can easily find and abuse their victims?

When are we going to talk about the many other types of sex trafficking manipulations going on?

There are forms of sex trafficking that aren't even being discussed yet, let alone identified by the anti-trafficking movement. Why is that?

The forms of sex trafficking include:
1. Child sex trafficking.
2. Religious sex trafficking.
3. Medical sex trafficking.
4. Mental health space sex trafficking.
5. Govermental sex trafficking.
6. Relationship sex trafficking.
7. Forced marriage sex trafficking.
8. Child marriage sex trafficking.
9. Organizational sex trafficking.
10. Anti-trafficking sex trafficking.
11. Academic sex trafficking.
12. Carceral system sex trafficking.
13. FAMILIAL SEX TRAFFICKING.
and more.

It's past time to question everything about the anti-trafficking movement.

They've had over 30 years since my first sex trafficking abuse ended and there are still no actual resources for sex trafficking victims and survivors. They save victims with cops, cuffs and criminalization and then sentence survivors to a lifetime of poverty.

When are we going to talk about sex trafficking beyond the propaganda marketing campaigns that only seek to raise funding?

When are we going to discuss rape/sex trafficking of young children? When are we going to save the 6 year olds being rape trafficked?

When are we going to create safe spaces where sex trafficking survivors feel safe to share or not share? Mental health support groups, emotional support hotlines, peer to peer support and other sex trafficking survivor community mental health services are absent.

Where are the safe spaces where we feel safe to ask for what we need and be trusted that if we ask for it, we need it?

Where is SURVIVOR centered support that is funded?

There is none, beyond what survivors ourselves have created. We reach out and beg community to support us and our wide, tangled webs of connecting to other sex trafficking victims and survivors. We beg the community to fund our survival while the anti-trafficking movement gets rich sending cops to cuff, coerce and criminalize us.

Why are survivors responsible for creating our own community care because the medical field hasn't bothered to talk to us?

Why are survivors responsible for creating our own care, while the anti-trafficking movement cuts off our access to funding also know as resources?

Why is the academic community largely talking about us without talking to us?

Where is all of the emergency Covid-19 funding that the anti-trafficking movement raised for victims/survivors? We haven't seen any of it.

What resources are there for sex trafficking survivors?

Resource available to sex trafficking survivors as of January 2021:

- referrals to lawyers to sue hotels instead of your sex trafficking abusers and rapists (a good diversion tactic...don't look at the abusers, look at the hotel)
- art therapy - which don't get me wrong, is great, in the right place at the right time. Survivors need access to survival before they can heal through art therapy. If we are thinking about how we are going to feed ourselves or where we can get a shower before we find a safe space to sleep outside or in a vehicle, we cannot enjoy the benefits art therapy can provide. We aren't surviving. How can we concentrate on art? Food, shelter, safety concerns all must be adequately addressed, according to the victims/survivors wishes. How many survivors are getting art therapy while houseless, sleeping in their vehicle?

I traced a human heart and sloshed some paint on it and blew on it and then I was offered some canned goods as I left the drop in center to sleep in a vehicle that wasn't even mine, because I don't own a vehicle.

Where is the anti-trafficking organizations who understand when someone is living in a vehicle, canned goods are not ideal for food. It's difficult to cook in a vehicle.

Where is the vehicle match up for survivors? Where's the organization who takes in vehicles, fixes them up and gives them to survivors? What about RVs? An RV for survivors program would be phenomenal. Where's these programs?

Where are the organizations that teach survivors how to drive or how to get vehicle insurance? Or how to shop for a vehicle? Or how to understand interest on vehicle loans?

Where is housing for survivors of all ages that is private? No shared rooms or bathrooms, no shelters, no forced shared living accommodations, where is it? Where is the room that only we have the ability to lock and unlock? This is paramount to the safety, security and comfort of many sex trafficking survivors.

We are a special kinda broken and if you want us to relax long enough to begin to start to heal, you need to center and listen to us. If we can't even relax, how do you expect us to heal?

Feed us a damn sandwich. Or whatever else we want to eat. Many sex trafficking survivors have special dietary needs. I won't ask anyone for anything. I might receive an offer if it is presented, but I certainly will not ask an anti-trafficking organization for anything.

-   yoga therapy - see comment for art therapy and apply it here also. It's hard to benefit from yoga therapy when you are in survival mode and don't know which bridge you are going to sleep under tonight.

-   **Why aren't our basic needs being met first? Why isn't there sex trafficking expert councilors for us to learn how to heal, survive, be ok and move on to thrive?**

Where are any personalized resources to fit the varying needs of sex trafficking victims/survivors? It's hard to benefit from art therapy when you are in survival mode.
Our basic needs aren't being met because the movement has been built from the top down. The folks at the top have no idea what it's like to be a sex trafficking victim or survivor. They stand at the top and raise funding for the folks at the bottom, while not providing any real resources to the folks they are raising funds for.

Anti-trafficking organizations are doing what they have the ability to do -- raise money and make it look like they are providing support.

But are they really? Or are they just raising funds to create an atmosphere that looks like help, but it's actually harmful to the very community they claim to be "helping"?

Cops, cuffs, coercion and criminalization are not what a resource looks like.

That doesn't being to cover the simple idea of why the fuck are cops arresting victims and treating them as abusers while not going after the abusers?

Question everything about the anti-trafficking movement.

If they keep raising funding for emergency shelters or drop in centers, ask them specifically for their resources list. They should be able to supply a PDF, photo or a printed list of resources available to survivors. I bet they don't have any resources beyond referrals that lead to nowhere...nowhere and maybe food banks.

An endless loop of referrals to call other referrals to call other referrals to call other referrals is not what resources are. It's the anti-trafficking movement sending you on a tail chasing adventure until you give up and stop looking for resources altogether.

Resources are, for example...

"So sorry you're going through this. I was there myself in 2018. How can I support you?"

And. Then. Do. Exactly. That.
Nothing more.
Nothing less.
Exactly That.

Regrettably, I called the local rape crisis hotline for sex trafficking victims/survivors, Pittsburgh Action Against Rape (PAAR). I was so rudely informed by the privileged white person on the other line, Etta, that I sound like I can navigate and find my own resources.

This person obviously has no idea what it's like to attempt to navigate your own resources in a time of need or crisis.

It is easier to navigate resources for someone else than it is for myself. I am always last in my own life. Centering my survival needs will always be hard for me. Sometimes I need people to advocate for my survival because I've given up. This happens a lot more than I allow others to see.

I hope that person never experiences abuse. If that person should experience abuse, if they reach out for support, I hope nobody ever tells them they can navigate their own resources.

How absolutely cruel to tell someone who calls a sex trafficking crisis line that they can navigate their own resources.

I was in a crisis. I needed Etta to advocate for me, not further harm me.

The most important step of supporting sex trafficking victims and survivors:

HOW CAN I SUPPORT YOU?

And then do that.

It is that simple.

Conquer one task and then move to the next. Yes, you might have to hold our hand. Yes, you might have to not touch us at all. Yes, you might only be able to communicate via text and utilize drop locations. Yes, you might never see our face or give us a hug or hold our hand. Yes you need to listen to us. Yes you need to support us.

We have been tokenized, exploited and removed from our survival resources.

Support starts with "How can I help you?"

If you're not ready to do that, then kindly exit your savior program now and save yourself the tears and pain. We know this hurts you too. It hurts us worse.

It's not a competition, survivors win by default. Our pain will always hurt us more than our pain will hurt people trying to "save" us.

Our support isn't about your needs. Our support is about fulfilling our needs. If you are unable to support others in their needs without centering you or your desires for that person, you might be doing it wrong. You might want to exit the harm reduction arena altogether.

Stop infantilizing sex trafficking victims and survivors. Our support is specific to our needs and has absolutely nothing to do with you. We don't need someone to treat us like a child, unless we request that, specifically.

At 10 years old, I knew what I needed. I needed safety, security and love. I had none of that.

If you become advocacy friends with your survivor friend, know that this will not be an easy road. We will probably never trust you, but that's ok, we will probably never trust anyone. Most days we question if we trust ourselves. Our lives have been permanently altered. And that's ok. We are a special kinda broken. We have unique and individual needs. And that's ok.

Support survivors exactly where we are and exactly how we wish to be supported, individually.

Healing from sex trafficking abuse is not a linear process. Sometimes we need hugs, sometimes we need space. And sometimes, we really just need to scream into the wind. It never stops hurting. Never.

Support us. Love us. Learn to communicate with your survivor friend.

I'm a special kinda broken. And that's ok.

Understand there is no book on how to heal from child sex

trafficking and how to move forward and live a life free from future abuses that was created with survivors.

Healing from sex trafficking is an individual process. There is no wrong way to heal. There is no wrong way to achieve safety and security in your life. There is no wrong way to move forward and choose to survive or take a chance to thrive.

Sadly, the medical, mental health and academic communities have yet to talk TO survivors about our abuse and the various aspects surrounding our abuse, our development during the abuse, our unique challenges and other important information that should be discussed. These communities have NO CLUE how to help sex trafficking survivors heal and not only survive but thrive.

Are we healing trauma by further abusing sex trafficking victims and survivors?

Are we healing trauma while allowing abusers to abuse survivors, further adding to their harm?

Are we allowing abusers to be in positions of power over survivors?

Are we "fixing" survivors by playing lab rat with them?

Where are sex trafficking survivors actual resources? Where are the millions in emergency COVID-19 funding they raised?

Where are our resources?

I am a childhood sex trafficking survivor who has spent almost 4 years looking for sex trafficking survivor support.

There is none, beyond survivor to survivor support.

Question everything about the

anti-trafficking movement.

Chapter Seven Summary

Abusers seek positions in which they can have power over and easily abuse their desired targets. This happens in families, organizations, harm reduction spaces and anywhere else abusers have easy access to abuse their perfect victim(s).

Stop saying children are confused when you really should be saying they were abused., h How can I support them?

How Can I Help?

How can I help you?

What can I do?

How can I support you?

When you are blue?

How can I stand by your side?

How can I help you survive the tide?

How can I hold your hand real tight?

How can I help you win the fight?

How can I abide?

Listen, learn and applied...

Help has been manipulated and tarnished

With consequences, survivors are garnished

Help is just a word people use

As they light the neverending fuse

Help has been twisted and redefined

Support suffocates while confined

Help doesn't exist in reality

Money grubbers, grubbing carefree

It's time to change the story

Support centered in all the glory

It's time to change the script

Money gatekeepers, they have slipped

It's time to fund folks directly

Provide beneficial support correctly

Stand up and speak the truth

Lack of resources is the proof

Stand up and speak of the misuse

Resources don't exist, it is abuse

Stand up and fund community

Stand together in unity

Stand up for real change

For the world we'll rearrange

HOW CAN I HELP?

Community support is what allows us to survive.

Here are a few ways you can support:

Helping survivors always starts with "How can I help you?"

Do that, nothing more, nothing less. Do exactly as a sex trafficking survivor requests. After you fulfill the first need, repeat the process. Do one thing at a time. Do not push survivors. Work on their timeline.

Respect boundaries.

You may have to help survivors navigate their own boundaries. This includes keeping yourself in check every step of the way. Survivors can define our own boundaries, sometimes we just need a little support. Sometimes we need a hug, others we need space.

Provide love and understanding.

Be there for survivors. Many survivors do not know how to experience love without strings. Often those strings are dipped in poison. Sometimes survivors simply do not know how to be loved or accept support.

Provide resources directly to survivors when able.

Most organizations set up to "help" sex trafficking survivors withhold resources from us. They then use the power of their resources to dictate the needs we have, instead of allowing us to decide our own needs. Many of these programs are created about us without any sex trafficking experts. I struggle all the time. I've been houseless recently. Obtaining my basic survival needs is hard for me. I sold my car to support our survivor led outreach program. We don't get paid. I beg on social media for money to fulfill outreach requests.

Sex trafficking survivors are struggling to survive. We are also the only ones providing real resources to our survivor siblings.

During the 2020 COVID-19 pandemic I couldn't find one anti-trafficking organization to send a specific pair of shoes to a sex trafficking victim so they could put the shoes on their feet and walk away from their abuser. They couldn't provide a specific pair of shoes for a neuro divergent sex trafficking victim? The shoes were less than $50. I begged on social media to raise the money for the shoes. The funds were raised within hours and the shoes were shipped the same day.

Why are sex trafficking survivors providing support for sex trafficking survivors, while the anti-trafficking movement gatekeeps our resources?

End Conflation - Save Lives

Sex trafficking is a form of rape.

Sex work is a form of work.

The two are *not* the same. End Conflation.

Provide direct support to survivors.

Survivor Siblings hosts a yearly survivors retreat that needs funding every October, we provide weekly and monthly and raise funding for sex trafficking victims to exit their abuse, we give cash directly to survivors.

Thanks for sending support! I appreciate you.

Without the support of community I would not survive.

Cash app $DearGabbyGFE

Cash, money orders, checks, gift cards, travel gift cards (train, bus, hotels, etc.) and more can be sent as applicable by later to:

Gabrielle Monroe

322 Mall Blvd #213

Monroeville, PA 15146

Patreon.com/GabrielleMonroe

If anyone is feeling extra generous and would like to buy me (or unload yours) a drivable *in good condition* RV so I have a vehicle and a home, I'd be forever grateful. A black Dodge Ram with a travel trailer is also a great option. Contact me on Twitter @AdvoGabby or send an email GabrielleMonroe@protonmail.com

You can also donate your travel rewards points directly to survivors. Sometimes we just need to get away, and we deserve to have resources to make that happen. If you'd like to donate your travel rewards, contact me at the above email.

call-to-action

Please call your state and national representatives Monday morning and ask them for the above legislation to protect children from sex trafficking. Google state Representative, state senator, nation senator, national representative and your city and state to find their contact info. Call and ask them to protect sex trafficking victims.

You have my permission to copy/paste, take a pictures, etc. and provide it to lawmakers directly.

1. National End Conflation Bill

2. State by State Amnesty for sex trafficking victims and sex workers

3. Full Decriminalization of prostitution and related offences for sex workers and clients of sex workers

Can you spare 5 minutes to Goolge your lawmakers and make a life saving call?

Thank You

Thank you for walking through my journey with me. I appreciate your valuable time.

Please remember your favorite self-care supports. This book is filled with trauma and questions. It is a lot. I know. Take care of you. Don't take on my pain. I am a Special Kinda Broken. I'll never be ok, and thats ok.

I am here. I survived.

Please pass along your book to the next reader. Protecting children is always above making profit.

Give it away, copy it, share this information.

We will never end childhood sex trafficking as long as we are tip-toeing around the hard conversations.

Let's have the hard conversations and collaborate to protect children from a horrible form of rape, known as sex trafficking.

Helping survivors always starts with "How can I help you?"

XO,

Gabby

Special Kinda Broken

Special Kinda Broken inside and out
I'll never be ok, I have no doubt

Innocence taken
They were not mistaken

They broke young little me
Broke so deep few understand or will ever see

They tested my will to live
My life to them I did give

They took the spark from my eye
All I wanted to do was die

They took my voice
They manipulated my choice

They took my fears
And caused my tears

They took my hope
I couldn't cope

They used my body for their sick game
 I would never, ever be the same

So young and hurt
Wanting to be 6 feet under the dirt

Destroy they must
They took my trust

They broke me deep
My soul they did keep

I'm a special Kinda broken
And that's ok

I'll never be ok
Not now or any other day

Special Kinda Broken up and down
The pain my tears will someday drown

Special Kinda Broken, I'll never be the same
I survived, I conquered their sick fucking game

SPECIAL KINDA BR♥KEN

We've all heard about sex trafficking
and the horrors that surround this
dehumanizing form of rape abuse.

Survivor Gabrielle Monroe lived
through child sex trafficking abuse,
grew up and broke the generational
sex trafficking, rape and sexual
abuse cycle in her family.

"I'm a special kinda broken, I'll
never be ok, and that's ok." ~
Gabrielle Monroe

Read as she recounts 7 stories of
abuse experienced at ages 9-10, how
the system failed her and what we
can do to end sex trafficking and
prevent child sex trafficking abuse.

About the Author
Gabrielle Monroe

Born and raised in small town
Greensburg, outside of Pittsburgh
Pennsylvania, Gabrielle Monroe
escaped abuse, grew up and created
a life she loves.
GabrielleMonroe.com

Made in the USA
Middletown, DE
01 October 2021